Steck Vaughn

Mastering MATH

Program Consultants

Robert Abbott
Assistant Director of Special Education
Waukegan Community Unit School District No. 60
Waukegan, Illinois

Marie Davis
Principal, McCoy Elementary School
Orange County Public Schools
Orlando, Florida

Monika Spindel
Mathematics Teacher
Austin, Texas

Suzanne H. Stevens
Specialist in Learning Disabilities
Learning Enhancement Consultant
Winston-Salem, North Carolina

Harcourt Achieve

Rigby • Steck-Vaughn

www.HarcourtAchieve.com
1.800.531.5015

Table of Contents

Acknowledgments
Illustration
Holly Cooper: pages 7, 57, 138   Barbara Corey: pages 11, 14, 15, 26, 30, 31, 46, 54, 55, 72, 73, 94, 95, 98, 101, 105, 119, 128, 129, 140, 141, 145, 148, 154   Judith duFour Love: pages 2, 3, 7, 13, 24, 25, 28, 29, 32, 33, 36, 52, 53, 58, 63, 65, 83, 84, 97, 103, 106, 143, 147, 150, 151 Laura Jackson: page 47   Maria Lyle: page 49 Lynn McClain: pages 24, 25, 148

Photography
P.1 ©Hunter Freeman/Tony Stone Images; p.3 CORBIS/Digital Stock; p.9 State Historical Society of Wisconsin; p.31 CORBIS/Digital Stock; p.33 ©Peter Beck/The Stock Market; p.71 ©Thomas Ives/The Stock Market; p.115 ©Robert Dammrich/ Tony Stone Images; p.137 ©David Young-Wolff/ PhotoEdit; Additional photography by: ©PhotoDisc.

CHAPTER 1

Adding and Subtracting Whole Numbers

▼ ▼ ▼ ▼ ▼ ▼ ▼

Angela volunteers to tell the class about her family's 2-week vacation trip. They drove 1,450 miles the first week and 1,376 miles the second week. How many miles in all did they drive?

Solve

▷ Write a problem about a trip you would like to take.

Place Value to Millions

Each digit in a number has a **value**. The value of a digit depends on its **place** in a number.

The value of the digit 2 in the number 2,345,876 is 2 million, or 2,000,000. It is in the millions' place.

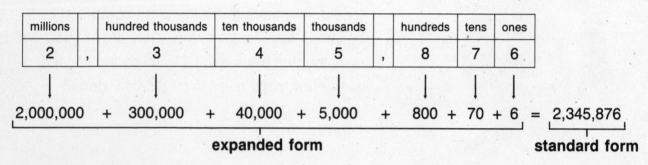

millions		hundred thousands	ten thousands	thousands		hundreds	tens	ones
2	,	3	4	5	,	8	7	6

2,000,000 + 300,000 + 40,000 + 5,000 + 800 + 70 + 6 = 2,345,876

expanded form · · · standard form

You read 2,345,876 as 2 million, 345 thousand, 876.

Guided Practice

▶Underline the digit in each number that is in the place shown. Then write the value of the underlined digit.

Place	Number	Value
1. millions	1,782,500	1,000,000
2. ten thousands	550,704	_____
3. hundred thousands	3,619,766	_____

▶Read each number. Then write it in standard form.

4. 7 million, 149 thousand, 300 _____

5. 5 million, 22 thousand, 15 _____

Practice

▷ Underline the digit in each number that is in the place shown. Then write the value of the underlined digit.

Place	Number	Value
1. tens	7,8 4 2	_____
2. thousands	1 3,7 5 0	_____
3. hundreds	9,6 3 1	_____
4. ten thousands	1 5 6,2 2 5	_____
5. millions	2,8 7 0,1 0 0	_____
6. hundred thousands	3,9 6 0,0 0 0	_____
7. millions	1,5 8 4,0 1 7	_____

▷ Write each number.

8. 7 thousand, 860 _____

9. 52 thousand, 575 _____

10. 160 thousand, 91 _____

11. 386 thousand _____

12. 4 million, 125 thousand, 600 _____

13. 2 million, 319 thousand, 952 _____

14. 9 million, 750 thousand, 125 _____

Using Math

▷ Chicago and Atlanta have the two busiest airports in the United States. In one year, there was a total of 1,517,988 takeoffs and landings at these airports. Circle the values of the two 1 digits in the number 1,517,988.

1,000,000   100,000   10,000   100   10   1

Adding 3- and 4-Digit Numbers

When you add, always begin by adding the digits in the ones' place.
Then add the digits in the tens', hundreds', and thousands' places.
Regroup when necessary.

```
1,7 2 3
+   4 2 7
←————————•
```

Step 1 Add the ones.	**Step 2** Add the tens.
``
      1
  1,723
+   427
      0
``` Regroup 10 ones as 1 ten 0 ones. | ```
      1
  1,723
+   427
     50
``` |
| **Step 3** Add the hundreds. | **Step 4** Add the thousands. |
| ```
   1 1
  1,723
+   427
    150
``` Regroup 11 hundreds as 1 thousand 1 hundred. | ```
   1 1
  1,723
+   427
  2,150
``` ← **sum** |

Guided Practice

▷Add.

1.	2.	3.	4.	5.
| ```
    1
  6 1 9
+8 2 5
─────
1,444
``` | ```
  5,4 1 9
+8,2 1 3
``` | ```
  4 0 8
+3 9 7
``` | ```
  1,9 3 6
+   2 8 4
``` | ```
  2,8 5 7
+4,7 6 4
``` |
```

Practice

▷ Add.

1. 456 +243	2. 269 +123	3. 717 +257	4. 546 +192	5. 825 +168
6. 2,651 + 284	7. 3,970 + 928	8. 4,201 +3,577	9. 1,389 +2,704	10. 5,672 +4,188
11. 4,331 +3,999	12. 6,990 +2,780	13. 2,127 +8,900	14. 9,314 +6,288	15. 7,543 +3,975

Using Math

▷ The Murphys are on a car trip. They left San Diego and drove to Los Angeles. Then they went to Santa Cruz. How many miles have the Murphys driven on their trip? Use the mileage chart to help you find the answer.

Work here.

The Murphys have driven _____ miles.

Mileage Chart		
From	To	Miles
San Diego	Los Angeles	127
Los Angeles	Santa Cruz	356
Santa Cruz	Eureka	357

Adding Large Numbers

When you add large numbers, line up the digits in their correct places.
If the digits are lined up correctly, it is easy to add.

Step 1 ▶ Add the ones.	Step 2 ▶ Add the tens.	Step 3 ▶ Add the hundreds.
146,345 + 27,192 —— 7	¹ 146,345 + 27,192 —— 37 Regroup 13 tens as 1 hundred 3 tens.	¹ 146,345 + 27,192 —— 537
Step 4 ▶ Add the thousands.	Step 5 ▶ Add the ten thousands.	Step 6 ▶ Add the hundred thousands.
¹ ¹ 146,345 + 27,192 —— 3,537 Regroup 13 thousands as 1 ten thousand 3 thousands.	¹ ¹ 146,345 + 27,192 —— 73,537	¹ ¹ 146,345 + 27,192 —— 173,537

Guided Practice

▶ Add.

1. ǀ ǀ
  17,851
+58,426
——
76,277
	2.
	  49,280
	+11,990
		3.
		  82,936
		+46,158
			4.
			  750,389
			+374,280

5.
  100,975
+ 19,259
	6.
	  647,300
	+184,200
		7.
		  586,204
		+156,596
			8.
			  750,389
			+374,280

6

Practice

▷ Add.

1. 1 4,5 2 8 + 1 2,4 5 2	2. 8 6,4 5 7 + 1 2,3 0 2	3. 5 1,8 3 6 + 3 4,5 2 9	4. 6 9 4,8 9 9 + 2 1 3,8 2 8
5. 4 6,6 2 5 + 3 1,7 9 7	6. 2 3,7 4 7 + 4 3,9 6 0	7. 9 7,8 7 5 + 1 2,0 4 5	8. 5 0 4,7 2 0 + 4 9 8,5 3 0
9. 5 2,8 1 4 + 7 9,2 0 9	10. 8 4,0 5 8 + 6 9,9 5 6	11. 1 4 2,7 3 0 + 3 7,2 5 0	12. 9 2 6,7 8 4 + 7 8 2,7 0 7
13. 3 4 3,7 6 3 + 6 5,6 9 7	14. 7 8 5,6 0 0 + 7 8,6 5 0	15. 2 0 5,6 3 0 + 7 4 6,2 9 7	16. 3 3 5,1 9 2 + 5 1 5,2 6 7

Using Math

▷ The most popular breeds of dogs are cocker spaniels and poodles. There are 96,396 cocker spaniels and 87,250 poodles registered in the United States. How many dogs are there registered for these two breeds?

Work here.

There are _____ dogs registered as cocker spaniels and poodles.

7

Subtracting 3- and 4-Digit Numbers

When you subtract, line up the digits in their correct places.
Begin by subtracting the ones. Regroup when necessary.

$$
\begin{array}{r}
1{,}2\,3\,6 \\
-\ \ 3\,5\,8 \\
\end{array}
$$

Step 1 Subtract the ones.

$$
\begin{array}{r}
{}^{2\ 16} \\
1{,}2\,\cancel{3}\,\cancel{6} \\
-\ \ 3\,5\,8 \\
\hline
8 \\
\end{array}
$$

Can you subtract 8 ones from 6 ones? No.

Regroup 3 tens 6 ones as 2 tens 16 ones.

Step 2 Subtract the tens.

$$
\begin{array}{r}
{}^{12} \\
{}^{1\ \cancel{2}\ 16} \\
1{,}2\,\cancel{3}\,\cancel{6} \\
-\ \ 3\,5\,8 \\
\hline
7\,8 \\
\end{array}
$$

Can you subtract 5 tens from 2 tens? No.

Regroup 2 hundreds 2 tens as 1 hundred 12 tens.

Step 3 Subtract the hundreds.

$$
\begin{array}{r}
{}^{11\ 12} \\
{}^{0\ \cancel{1}\ \cancel{2}\ 16} \\
\cancel{1}{,}\cancel{2}\,\cancel{3}\,\cancel{6} \\
-\ \ 3\,5\,8 \\
\hline
8\,7\,8 \\
\end{array}
$$

Can you subtract 3 hundreds from 1 hundred? No.

Regroup 1 thousand 1 hundred as 11 hundreds.

There are no thousands left to subtract.

Check your answer by adding.

$$
\begin{array}{r}
{}^{1\ 1} \\
3\,5\,8 \\
+\,8\,7\,8 \\
\hline
1{,}2\,3\,6 \\
\end{array}
$$

Guided Practice

▷ Subtract.

1. $\begin{array}{r}{}^{\ \ 10}\\{}^{7\ \cancel{0}\ 12}\\ \cancel{8}\,\cancel{1}\,\cancel{2}\\ -3\,4\,7\\ \hline 4\,6\,5\end{array}$	2. $\begin{array}{r}5\,7\,9\\ -4\,8\,1\\ \hline \end{array}$	3. $\begin{array}{r}1{,}7\,3\,1\\ -\ \ 8\,1\,9\\ \hline \end{array}$	4. $\begin{array}{r}4{,}3\,8\,3\\ -3{,}9\,9\,2\\ \hline \end{array}$	5. $\begin{array}{r}6{,}4\,3\,1\\ -1{,}7\,5\,6\\ \hline \end{array}$

Practice

Subtract.

1.   439
  −212
	2. 882
	  −536
		3. 619
		  −565
			4. 734
			  −296
				5. 8,500
				 −4,700

6.   396
  −188
	7. 560
	  −190
		8. 917
		  −348
			9. 834
			  −789
				10. 5,672
				 −2,385

11. 2,595 − 680	12. 4,713 − 543	13. 1,230 − 853	14. 6,458 − 234	15. 3,344 −1,895
16. 5,761 −3,552	17. 9,430 −2,597	18. 8,265 −7,765	19. 7,567 −7,498	20. 2,863 − 476

Using Math

Abraham Lincoln was born in 1809. He became the 16th president of the United States in 1861. How old was Lincoln when he became president?

Lincoln was _____ years old when he became president.

Work here.

9

Subtracting From Zeros

When you subtract from a number that has no ones, tens, or hundreds, you need to regroup more than once before subtracting.

 · ← You must regroup to the thousands' place.

16,000
− 2,328

Step 1 Regroup the thousands.

6 thousands = 5 thousands 10 hundreds

$\overset{5\ 10}{1\ \cancel{6},\cancel{0}\ 0\ 0}$

Step 2 Regroup the hundreds.

10 hundreds = 9 hundreds 10 tens

$\overset{\ \ \ 9}{\overset{5\ 1\cancel{0}\ 10}{1\ \cancel{6},\cancel{0}\ 0\ 0}}$

Step 3 Regroup the tens.

10 tens = 9 tens 10 ones

$\overset{\ \ \ 9\ 9}{\overset{5\ 1\cancel{0}\ 1\cancel{0}\ 10}{1\ \cancel{6},\cancel{0}\ \cancel{0}\ \cancel{0}}}$

Now subtract.

$$\begin{array}{r} \overset{\ \ \ \ 9\ 9}{\overset{5\ 10\ 10\ 10}{1\ \cancel{6},\cancel{0}\ \cancel{0}\ \cancel{0}}} \\ -\ \ \ 2,3\ 2\ 8 \\ \hline 1\ 3,6\ 7\ 2 \end{array}$$ ← difference

Check:

$$\begin{array}{r} \overset{1\ 11}{2,3\ 2\ 8} \\ +13,672 \\ \hline 16,000 \end{array}$$

Guided Practice

▷ Subtract.

1. $\overset{\ \ \ \ \ 9\ 9}{\overset{2\ 10\ 10\ 16}{3,\cancel{0}\ \cancel{0}\ \cancel{6}}}$ $-1,9\ 2\ 8$ $\overline{1,078}$	2. $52,004$ $-29,637$	3. 900 -453	4. $800,500$ $-426,195$
5. $29,000$ $-26,367$	6. 400 -158	7. $570,000$ $-356,177$	8. $96,400$ $-7,628$

10

Practice

▷ Subtract.

1.   800
  −663
	2. 500
	  −194
		3. 700
		  −382
			4. 48,000
			  −45,895

5.   4,000
  −2,563
	6. 1,000
	  − 486
		7. 8,003
		  −5,928
			8. 124,000
			  − 31,429

9.   6,000
  −5,345
	10. 7,002
	  −1,256
		11. 5,000
		  −2,889
			12. 300,700
			  −164,283

13.   17,000
  − 9,142
	14. 82,005
	  −31,758
		15. 40,000
		  −17,167
			16. 60,000
			  −45,826

Using Math

▷ The longest river in South America is the Amazon River. It is 4,000 miles long. The longest river in North America is the Mississippi River. It is 2,340 miles long. What is the difference in the length of the two rivers?

Work here.

The difference in the length of the two rivers is _____ miles.

11

Estimating Sums and Differences

You round numbers to find out **about** how many.

To round a number, follow these steps.

Round 1,742 to the nearest hundred.

Step 1	Underline the place you are rounding to.	1,7 4 2
Step 2	Circle the next digit to the right.	1,7④2
Step 3	If the circled digit is **less than 5**, round down. If the circled digit is **5 or more**, round up.	1,7 0 0

You can **estimate** the sum or difference of a problem by rounding.
An estimate is close to the exact answer.

Round to the nearest **hundred** to estimate the sum.	Round to the nearest **thousand** to estimate the difference.
1,362 ⟶ 1,400 round up + 828 ⟶ + 800 round down 2,200 ⟵ estimate	48,567 ⟶ 49,000 round up − 13,045 ⟶ − 13,000 round down 36,000 ⟵ estimate

Guided Practice

▷ Estimate each sum or difference by rounding the numbers to the place shown.

1.	**Nearest Hundred**	2.	**Nearest Thousand**
7,4 9 7 ⟶ 7,500 + 8 7 3 ⟶ + 9 0 0 8,4 0 0		2 7,8 5 5 ⟶ − 1 6,2 7 2 ⟶ −	

Practice

▷ Estimate each sum or difference by rounding to the nearest **hundred**.

1.	2.	3.
372 +205 + _____	1,452 + 735 + _____	8,939 +5,093 + _____

4.	5.	6.
659 −172 − _____	9,425 − 382 − _____	5,208 −2,759 − _____

▷ Estimate each sum or difference by rounding to the nearest **thousand**.

7.	8.	9.
8,580 +7,204 + _____	43,389 + 3,526 + _____	27,885 +16,348 + _____

10.	11.	12.
7,584 −3,033 − _____	81,247 −76,803 − _____	95,532 −79,253 − _____

Using Math

▷ Ed scored 2,872 points on a computer game. Ava scored 3,515. Ed rounded the sum of their points to the nearest thousand. Ava rounded to the nearest hundred.

Work here.

Whose estimate was closer to the actual sum? _____

The Fahrenheit Scale

We use a **thermometer** to measure temperature. A **Fahrenheit** thermometer measures temperatures in degrees Fahrenheit. We write degrees Fahrenheit as °**F**. Water freezes at 32°F and boils at 212°F.

The liquid in the thermometer helps us read the temperature. As the temperature gets warmer, the liquid in the thermometer rises.

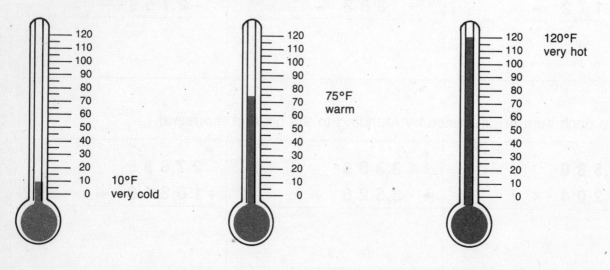

Guided Practice

▶Write the degrees Fahrenheit for each thermometer. Then ring the kind of day each temperature means.

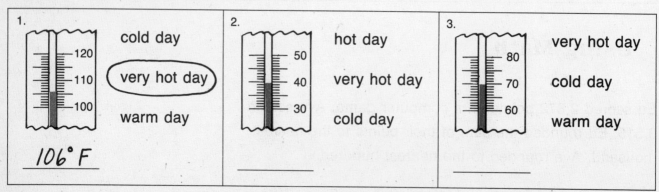

1.
cold day
very hot day
warm day

106°F

2.
hot day
very hot day
cold day

3.
very hot day
cold day
warm day

Practice

▶Ring the correct temperature.

1. The soup in a pot begins to boil. 12°F 100°F 212°F	2. You might go swimming at the beach. 35°F 50°F 80°F
3. You can go ice skating on the pond. 15°F 55°F 80°F	4. You can go outside without a coat. 0°F 32°F 65°F
5. A tray of ice cubes freezes. 32°F 46°F 92°F	6. You play baseball with your friends. 12°F 73°F 210°F
7. The trees begin to lose their leaves. 0°F 35°F 178°F	8. There is snow on the sidewalk. 25°F 54°F 63°F
9. You need to wear a heavy coat. 30°F 80°F 100°F	10. You bake granola bars. 40°F 85°F 350°F

Using Math

▶On June 6, the temperature in Arizona was 100°F. On the same day, the temperature in Maine was 55°F. Color in the thermometers to show the temperature for each state.

What was the difference in temperatures between the two states?

The difference was _____.

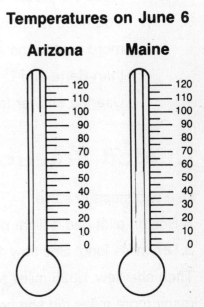

Temperatures on June 6

Arizona   **Maine**

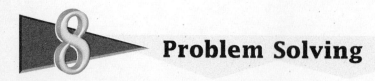

Problem Solving

Two-Step Problems

Yogi Berra hit 358 home runs in his professional baseball career. Joe DiMaggio hit 361 home runs. Hank Aaron hit 755 home runs. How many more home runs did Hank Aaron hit than Berra and DiMaggio hit together?

> This is a two-step problem.
> You will use more than one operation to solve it.

Step 1   Read the problem to find what you need first.

You need to know the number of home runs in all that Berra and DiMaggio hit.

Solve for that part.

$$\begin{array}{r} 358 \\ + 361 \\ \hline 719 \end{array} \text{ home runs}$$

Step 2   Read the problem to find what you need next.

You need to know how many more home runs Aaron hit than Berra and DiMaggio together.

Use the answer from Step 1 to solve.

$$\begin{array}{r} 755 \\ - 719 \\ \hline 36 \end{array} \text{ more home runs}$$

Guided Practice

▷ Use two steps to solve.

A Boston pilot had a flight plan that was 3,127 miles long. She flew 1,557 miles to Dallas. Then she flew 1,025 miles to Cleveland. How many more miles did she have left to fly?

Step 1	Step 2
$\begin{array}{r} 1,557 \\ + 1,025 \\ \hline 2,582 \text{ miles} \end{array}$	$\begin{array}{r} 3,127 \\ - 2,582 \\ \hline 545 \text{ miles left} \end{array}$

Practice

▷ Use two steps to solve.

	Step 1	Step 2
1. A company has 362 workers. 172 of them work in sales. 155 people work in the main office. The other workers are in advertising. How many company workers are in advertising?		workers
2. Mr. Santeria was reading a book that has 287 pages. He read 128 pages last month and 135 pages this month. How many pages did Mr. Santeria have left to read?		pages
3. Brian had 246 rare coins. Carmen had 69 fewer rare coins than Brian had. Jasmine had 51 more rare coins than Carmen had. How many rare coins did Jasmine have?		coins
4. Afton drove 3,163 miles from Boston to Seattle. First he drove 1,188 miles to St. Louis. Then he drove 858 miles to Denver. How many more miles did Afton drive to get to Seattle?		miles
5. President Bill Clinton was born in 1946. He became president 46 years later. George Washington became president 203 years before Clinton did. In what year did George Washington become president?		year

▷ Underline the digit in each number that is in the place shown. Then write the value of the underlined digit.   pages 2–3

Place	Number	Value
1. millions	4,9 3 5,0 0 0	_____
2. hundred thousands	7,5 6 9,3 2 2	_____
3. ten thousands	8,0 2 6,4 7 5	_____

▷ Write each number.   pages 2–3

4. 4 thousand, 852 _____   5. 124 thousand, 65 _____

6. 5 million, 63 thousand, 450 _____

▷ Add.

pages 4–5

7. 463 +129	8. 982 +950	9. 2,507 + 991	10. 4,065 +2,294

pages 6–7

11. 13,475 +13,915	12. 134,548 + 47,325	13. 228,005 + 99,236	14. 649,710 +519,850

▷ Subtract.   pages 8–9

15. 328 −155	16. 714 −246	17. 2,972 − 980	18. 8,482 −2,886

 **CHAPTER** **Review**

▶ Subtract.   pages 10–11

19.	20.	21.	22.
6 0 0 − 4 8 6	5,0 0 6 − 2,6 4 7	7 0,0 0 0 − 2 5,3 9 2	4 0 0,8 0 0 − 2 5 3,7 9 4

▶ Estimate each sum by rounding to the nearest **hundred**.   pages 12–13

23. 5 1 7 ⟶ + 4 9 1 ⟶ + _____	24. 3,8 5 6 ⟶ + 4 4 6 ⟶ + _____

▶ Estimate each difference by rounding to the nearest **thousand**.   pages 12–13

25. 8,5 9 8 ⟶ − 2,8 9 4 ⟶ − _____	26. 1 7,3 8 1 ⟶ − 4,0 9 4 ⟶ − _____

▶ Ring the correct temperature.   pages 14–15

27. A puddle turns to ice. 32°F 62°F 102°F	28. The local swimming pool opens. 15°F 42°F 75°F
29. The heat in the school is turned on. 62°F 86°F 110°F	30. The water in a pot begins to boil. 12°F 102°F 212°F

19

Use two steps to solve.
pages 16–17

	Step 1	Step 2
31. Sonya had a box of 500 envelopes. She used 189 envelopes for employee checks. She used 215 envelopes to mail letters. How many envelopes does she have left?		envelopes
32. There are 365 days in a year. Luis went to school 185 days this year. He worked at a summer job for 50 days. How many days did Luis have away from school and work during the year?		days
33. Robin went on a trip with $672 to spend. She spent $278 on hotel rooms. Her meals cost a total of $203. How much money did Robin have left that she could spend on other things?		
34. Stan sold 243 rodeo tickets on Monday. He sold 155 tickets on Tuesday. Then he sold 171 tickets on Wednesday. How many tickets in all did Stan sell on these days?		tickets
35. Ricco bought 467 boards to build a fence. Then he bought 108 more boards for the fence. When he finished building the fence, Ricco had used 526 boards. How many boards were left?		boards

▷ Write each number.

1. 374 thousand, 842 _____

2. 6 million, 250 thousand, 65 _____

▷ Add.

3.   6 1 8
    +1 9 8
	4. 3,8 7 4
	    +2,6 4 6
		5. 3 4,5 9 0
		    +6 1,8 4 0
			6. 1 6 4,7 9 6
			    + 5 8,6 0 2

▷ Subtract.

7.   7 2 4
    −2 8 6
	8. 4,8 3 6
	    −3,7 7 8
		9. 5,0 0 0
		    −1,4 2 7
			10. 9 0,0 0 8
			    −3 8,5 6 2

▷ Estimate each sum or difference by rounding the numbers to the place shown.

11. **Nearest Hundred**	12. **Nearest Thousand**

5,7 4 2 ⟶
    +2,3 8 9 ⟶   + _____
	6 2,6 3 7 ⟶
	    −1 8,5 4 6 ⟶ − _____

▷ Ring the correct temperature.

| 13. A fruit bar will freeze.

      32°F   62°F   102°F | 14. The water for a cup of tea boils.

      21°F   96°F   212°F |

▷ Use two steps to solve.

	Step 1	Step 2
15. Mr. Bingham bought 268 pounds of meat for the company cookout. They cooked 175 pounds of chicken. They cooked 84 pounds of hamburger. How many pounds of meat were not cooked?		pounds
16. Shayla made 439 hair bows to sell at a craft show. She sold 325 bows in a day. She went home that night and made 306 more bows. How many bows did Shayla have then?		bows
17. Rick's history paper was 352 words long. Cindy's paper had 108 words, and Ray's paper had 170 words. How many words longer was Rick's paper than Cindy's and Ray's papers together?		words
18. Lin drove 107 miles from his house to pick up his sister. Then he drove 58 miles more to his grandmother's house. Later he drove back to his sister's house. How many miles in all had Lin driven then?		miles
19. Sally worked 275 hours last summer at Camp Bergen. Cole worked 54 hours less than Sally. Fili worked 63 hours more than Cole. How many hours did Fili work last summer?		hours

2 Multiplying and Dividing Whole Numbers

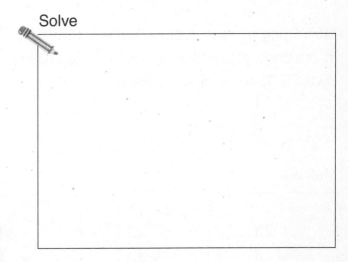

Baytown Movie Theater has 5 theaters. Each theater has 64 balcony seats. How many balcony seats in all are there?

Solve

▷ Write your own problem about seats in a theater.

Multiplying by Ones and Tens

One cassette case holds 24 tapes. How many tapes can 6 cases hold?
Multiply 24 by 6 to find the answer.

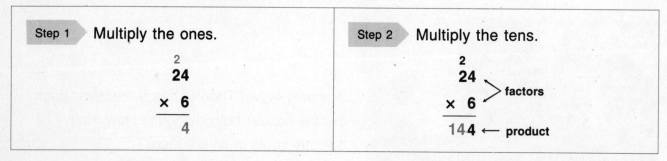

Step 1 ▸ Multiply the ones.

$$\begin{array}{r} 2 \\ 24 \\ \times\ 6 \\ \hline 4 \end{array}$$

Step 2 ▸ Multiply the tens.

$$\begin{array}{r} 2 \\ 24 \\ \times\ 6 \\ \hline 144 \end{array}$$

factors

144 ← product

Six cases can hold 144 tapes.

Multiplying by tens is easy. Write a zero
in the ones' place to show you are multiplying
by tens. Then multiply by the tens' digit.

$$\begin{array}{r} 2 \\ 24 \\ \times 60 \\ \hline 1{,}440 \end{array}$$

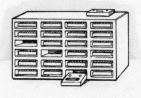

Guided Practice

▸ Multiply.

1. $\begin{array}{r} 1 \\ 23 \\ \times\ 4 \\ \hline 92 \end{array}$	2. $\begin{array}{r} 1 \\ 23 \\ \times 40 \\ \hline 920 \end{array}$	3. $\begin{array}{r} 81 \\ \times\ 7 \\ \hline \end{array}$	4. $\begin{array}{r} 81 \\ \times 70 \\ \hline \end{array}$	5. $\begin{array}{r} 26 \\ \times 60 \\ \hline \end{array}$
6. $\begin{array}{r} 54 \\ \times\ 3 \\ \hline \end{array}$	7. $\begin{array}{r} 54 \\ \times 30 \\ \hline \end{array}$	8. $\begin{array}{r} 97 \\ \times\ 5 \\ \hline \end{array}$	9. $\begin{array}{r} 42 \\ \times 80 \\ \hline \end{array}$	10. $\begin{array}{r} 35 \\ \times 50 \\ \hline \end{array}$

Practice

Multiply.

1. 38 × 2	2. 38 × 20	3. 17 × 5	4. 46 × 6	5. 14 × 20
6. 29 × 3	7. 29 × 30	8. 42 × 7	9. 96 × 5	10. 65 × 10
11. 45 × 2	12. 45 × 20	13. 28 × 8	14. 59 × 9	15. 52 × 50
16. 72 × 9	17. 72 × 90	18. 98 × 4	19. 69 × 8	20. 86 × 40

Using Math

Cars waiting to get on the ferry were placed in 4 lines. If 17 cars were in each line, how many cars were going on the ferry?

Work here.

There were _____ cars going on the ferry.

Multiplying by 2-Digit Numbers

Jordon's had a sale. All sunglasses were half-price.

The store sold an average of 617 pairs a day.

How many pairs were sold in 42 days?

Three steps are needed to multiply 617 by 42.

Step 1 ▶ Multiply 617 by 2 ones.	Step 2 ▶ Multiply 617 by 4 tens.	Step 3 ▶ Add.
¹ 6 1 7 × 4 2 _____ 1 2 3 4 ← 2 × 617 = 1234	² 1̶ 6 1 7 × 4 2 _____ 1 2 3 4 2 4 6 8 0 ← 40 × 617 = 24680 **Remember to write the 0 in the ones' place.**	² 1̶ 6 1 7 × 4 2 _____ 1 2 3 4 +2 4 6 8 0 _____ 2 5,9 1 4 Place the comma.

Guided Practice

▶ Multiply.

1. ² 67 ×14 _____ 268 +670 _____ 938	2. 82 ×15	3. 374 × 16	4. 163 × 23	5. 467 × 35

Practice

▷ Multiply.

1. 31 × 11	2. 52 × 12	3. 66 × 14	4. 50 × 19	5. 38 × 23
6. 48 × 26	7. 79 × 17	8. 89 × 43	9. 146 × 11	10. 316 × 13
11. 427 × 14	12. 263 × 21	13. 582 × 32	14. 298 × 98	15. 894 × 54

Using Math

▷ There are 365 days in a year. If Bob were awake 16 hours every day, how many hours would he be awake in one year?

Work here.

Bob would be awake _____ hours in one year.

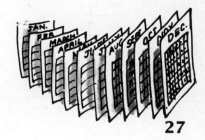

27

1-Digit Divisors

Beth and Scott picked a total of 37 cherries.
Can they share the cherries equally?

Divide 37 by 2 to find the answer.

divisor → 2)37 ← dividend

Step 1 ▶ Divide the tens.	Step 2 ▶ Divide the ones.
Divide $3 \div 2$ Write one in the tens' place. **Multiply** 1×2 **Subtract** $3 - 2$ **Compare** Is 1 less than 2? Yes. Go on to Step 2.	**Bring down** the 7. **Divide** $17 \div 2$ Write 8 in the ones' place. **Multiply** 8×2 **Subtract** $17 - 16$ Write the remainder with the quotient.

$$\begin{array}{r} 1 \\ 2\overline{)37} \\ -2 \\ \hline 1 \end{array}$$

$$\begin{array}{r} 1\,8 \text{ R1} \leftarrow \text{quotient} \\ 2\overline{)37} \\ -2\downarrow \\ \hline 17 \\ -16 \\ \hline 1 \leftarrow \text{remainder} \end{array}$$

When the cherries are divided equally, each person gets 18 cherries.
There is 1 cherry left over.

Guided Practice

▷ Divide.

1. $\begin{array}{r} 21 \text{ R3} \\ 4\overline{)87} \\ -8 \\ \hline 07 \\ -4 \\ \hline 3 \end{array}$	2. $3\overline{)69}$	3. $7\overline{)98}$	4. $5\overline{)61}$

Practice

Divide.

1. 4)47	2. 3)88	3. 2)52	4. 4)49
5. 6)86	6. 5)75	7. 9)99	8. 2)79
9. 3)84	10. 8)99	11. 7)96	12. 3)98

Problem Solving

Use two steps to solve.

Chi went on a 342-mile trip. She drove
178 miles in the morning. She drove
127 miles in the afternoon. How many more
miles does Chi have left to drive?

Step 1	Step 2
+ _____	− _____
	miles

1-Digit Divisors

Sometimes you need to go to the second digit in the dividend to begin dividing.

$$5\overline{)203}$$

Can you divide 2 by 5? No. ⌐

Can you divide 20 by 5? Yes. ⌐

Step 1 ▷ Divide the tens.

Divide $20 \div 5$

   Write the 4 over the 0.

   This is the tens' place.

Multiply 4×5

Subtract $20 - 20$

Compare $0 < 5$

$$\begin{array}{r} 4 \\ 5\overline{)203} \\ -20 \\ \hline 0 \end{array}$$

Step 2 ▷ Divide the ones.

Bring down the 3.

   Can you divide 3 by 5? No.

   Write a 0 over the 3.

   This is the ones' place.

Multiply 0×5

Subtract $3 - 0$

   Write the remainder with the quotient.

$$\begin{array}{r} 40 \text{ R}3 \\ 5\overline{)203} \\ -20 \\ \hline 03 \\ -0 \\ \hline 3 \end{array}$$

Guided Practice

▷ Divide.

1. $\begin{array}{r} 64 \\ 6\overline{)384} \\ -36 \\ \hline 24 \\ -24 \\ \hline 0 \end{array}$	2. $4\overline{)323}$	3. $8\overline{)418}$	4. $5\overline{)250}$

Practice

▷ Divide.

1. $3\overline{)126}$	2. $2\overline{)155}$	3. $7\overline{)216}$	4. $5\overline{)405}$
5. $7\overline{)579}$	6. $4\overline{)363}$	7. $6\overline{)498}$	8. $8\overline{)261}$
9. $4\overline{)242}$	10. $9\overline{)856}$	11. $5\overline{)350}$	12. $2\overline{)109}$

Using Math

▷ The airplane flying from Chicago to Houston has 133 passengers. There are 6 seats in each row of the airplane. How many rows can be completely filled?

Work here.

_____ rows can be completely filled.

2-Digit Divisors

Rounding a 2-digit divisor to the nearest ten can help you find the quotient.

Divide 674 by 29.   29)674

⌐Round up to 30.⌐

Step 1 Divide the tens.		**Step 2** Divide the ones.	
Divide 67 ÷ 29	2$$	**Bring down** the 4.	23 R7
Think 67 ÷ 30	29)674	**Divide** 94 ÷ 29	29)674
6 ÷ 3 = 2	$\,-58$	Think 94 ÷ 30	$\,-58$
Write the 2 over the 7.	9	9 ÷ 3	94
Multiply 2 × 29		Write the 3 over the 4.	$\,-87$
Subtract 67 − 58		**Multiply** 3 × 29	7
Compare 9 < 29		**Subtract** 94 − 87	
		Compare 7 < 29	
		Write the remainder with the quotient.	

Guided Practice

▷Divide.

1. $\quad$ 24 32)768 $\,-64$ $\overline{128}$ $\,-128$ $\overline{0}$	2. $\quad$ 19)74	3. $\quad$ 12)361	4. $\quad$ 18)225

32

Practice

▷ Divide.

1. 31)69	2. 11)55	3. 18)83	4. 29)94
5. 19)425	6. 51)586	7. 32)992	8. 28)689
9. 81)823	10. 19)512	11. 22)792	12. 65)885

Using Math

▷ Jamie collected 483 empty cans for recycling. She put 21 cans in each bag. How many bags did she use?

Work here.

Jamie used_____ bags.

33

Adjusting the Quotient

Sometimes you need to change a digit in the quotient when dividing.

Divide 86 by 17.   17)86

Step 1 17)86	Step 2 4 17)86 – 68 18	Step 3 5 R1 17)86 – 85 1
Round up to 20. Think: 86 ÷ 20 8 ÷ 2 = 4	Compare: 18 > 17 Try the next larger number.	Compare: 1 < 17 The quotient is correct.

Divide 126 by 64.   64)126

Step 1 64)126	Step 2 2 64)126 – 128	Step 3 1 R62 64)126 – 64 62
Round down to 60. Think 126 ÷ 60 12 ÷ 6 = 2	Compare: 128 > 126 You cannot subtract. Try the next smaller number.	Compare: 62 < 64 The quotient is correct.

Guided Practice

▷ Divide.

1. 6 12)72 –72 0	2. 26)164	3. 34)496	4. 15)657

34

Practice

▷ Divide.

1. $13\overline{)79}$	2. $26\overline{)53}$	3. $15\overline{)82}$	4. $33\overline{)96}$
5. $17\overline{)425}$	6. $22\overline{)816}$	7. $26\overline{)230}$	8. $38\overline{)266}$
9. $54\overline{)967}$	10. $16\overline{)926}$	11. $42\overline{)807}$	12. $25\overline{)754}$

Using Math

▷ Mr. Ford's class received 145 tickets for the Country Fair. He gave each of his 23 students an equal number of tickets. Sarah is a student in the class. She told her family she could get 7 tickets. Was she correct?

Work here.

Circle **yes** or **no**.   Yes   No

35

Inches, Feet, Yards, and Miles

Inches, **feet**, **yards**, and **miles** are units to measure **length** or **distance**.

A button is 1 inch across.

A hammer is about 1 foot long.

A baseball bat is about 1 yard long.

Longer distances are measured in **miles**.

It takes Sally about 15 minutes to walk 1 mile to school.

> 12 inches = 1 foot
> 36 inches = 1 yard
> 3 feet = 1 yard
> 5,280 feet = 1 mile

To change lengths to a smaller unit, such as yards to feet, multiply.	To change lengths to a larger unit, such as feet to yards, divide.
2 yards = ___?___ feet	6 feet = ___?___ yards
$2 \times 3 = 6$ feet	$6 \div 3 = 2$ yards
└ 3 feet = 1 yard ┘	└ 3 feet = 1 yard ┘

Guided Practice

▷ Ring the unit of measure you would use.

1. a table	2. a notebook	3. a football field
(yard) mile	foot yard	inch yard

▷ Complete.

4. 2 feet = __24__ inches   5. 36 inches = _____ yard

6. 15 feet = _____ yards   7. 1 mile = _____ feet

36

Practice

Ring the best length or distance.

1. distance of a bus ride 5 feet 5 miles	2. length of a sheet of notebook paper 11 inches 11 feet
3. length of a swimming pool 15 inches 15 yards	4. height of a house 20 feet 20 miles

Complete.

5. 7 yards = _____ feet

6. 144 inches = _____ feet

7. 180 inches = _____ yards

8. 5 feet = _____ inches

9. 174 feet = _____ yards

10. 2 miles = _____ feet

Using Math

Carmen bought 5 yards of ribbon. She is going to make 1-inch red tags for the students to wear on graduation day. How many 1-inch tags can Carmen make?

Work here.

Carmen can make _____ 1-inch ribbon tags.

Problem Solving

Two-Step Problems

Melissa has 32 color pencils in her art kit.

Melissa has 2 times more color pencils than Juan has.

Carlos has 3 times more color pencils than Juan has.

How many color pencils does Carlos have?

> This is a two-step problem.
>
> You will use more than one operation to solve it.

Step 1 Read the problem to find what you need first.

You need to know how many

color pencils Juan has.

Solve for that part.

```
      16   Juan's pencils
  2 ) 32
     - 2
      12
     - 12
       0
```

Step 2 Read the problem to see what you need next.

You need to know how many

color pencils Carlos has.

Use the answer from Step 1 to solve.

```
    16
  ×  3
    48   Carlos' pencils
```

Guided Practice

▷ Use two steps to solve.

Quinton had 450 pennies. He spent
100 pennies at a garage sale. Then
he rolled the pennies he had left.
He put 50 pennies in each roll.
How many rolls of pennies did Quinton have?

Step 1	Step 2
450 − 100 350	7 rolls 50) 350 − 350

38

Practice

▷ Use two steps to solve.

	Step 1	Step 2
1. Kendray shared 32 apples equally with 8 friends. Two of her friends made pies with the apples they got from Kendray. How many apples in all were used for pies?		apples
2. Phil got 2 cookies for 50 cents. How much money would he have spent for 3 cookies?		cents
3. Coach MacKenzie needs 45 students for 5 baseball teams. How many students would he need for 8 baseball teams?		students
4. At Video To Go it takes 240 video tapes to fill 10 shelves. How many tapes would fill 16 shelves?		videos
5. At the state fair, Perry used 24 tickets on 6 rides. Each ride cost the same number of tickets. How many more tickets will Perry use if he rides 3 more rides?		tickets

39

Review

▶ Multiply.

pages 24–25				
1. $\begin{array}{r} 34 \\ \times\ 2 \\ \hline \end{array}$	2. $\begin{array}{r} 34 \\ \times 20 \\ \hline \end{array}$	3. $\begin{array}{r} 65 \\ \times\ 3 \\ \hline \end{array}$	4. $\begin{array}{r} 65 \\ \times 30 \\ \hline \end{array}$	5. $\begin{array}{r} 78 \\ \times 50 \\ \hline \end{array}$
pages 26–27				
6. $\begin{array}{r} 76 \\ \times 13 \\ \hline \end{array}$	7. $\begin{array}{r} 28 \\ \times 22 \\ \hline \end{array}$	8. $\begin{array}{r} 95 \\ \times 36 \\ \hline \end{array}$	9. $\begin{array}{r} 159 \\ \times\ 18 \\ \hline \end{array}$	10. $\begin{array}{r} 265 \\ \times\ 23 \\ \hline \end{array}$

▶ Divide.

pages 28–29			
11. $7\overline{)79}$	12. $4\overline{)68}$	13. $2\overline{)95}$	14. $3\overline{)68}$
pages 30–31			
15. $2\overline{)164}$	16. $5\overline{)352}$	17. $6\overline{)505}$	18. $9\overline{)859}$

▷ Divide.

pages 32–33 19. 12)48	20. 39)85	21. 63)976	22. 28)654
pages 34–35 23. 17)98	24. 34)129	25. 83)243	26. 73)875
27. 15)643	28. 14)560	29. 26)813	30. 32)902

▷ Complete. pages 36–37

31. 252 inches = _____ yards

32. 3 feet = _____ inches

33. 36 feet = _____ yards

34. 2 yards = _____ inches

35. 72 inches = _____ feet

36. 5,280 feet = _____ mile

▶Use two steps to solve.
pages 38–39

	Step 1	Step 2
37. It took Erin 55 minutes to finish 5 math problems. How long will it take her to finish 8 problems of the same kind?		minutes
38. Miko can fit 246 files in 3 drawers. How many files can she fit in 7 drawers?		files
39. Jerome had 137 rocks in a rock collection. He gave 13 rocks away. Then he put the rocks into 4 equal groups. How many rocks did Jerome put in each group?		rocks
40. Mr. Hanson had 24 students in his class. Ms. Sing had 31 students in her class. The classes went on a fossil-hunting field trip. Each student found 7 fossils. How many fossils did the students find altogether?		fossils
41. Marla bought 4 video tapes. Each tape cost $18. She also bought a television for $197. How much money did Marla spend?		

Multiply.

1. 32 × 3	2. 76 × 30	3. 27 × 12	4. 78 × 23	5. 325 × 26

Divide.

6. 2)68	7. 5)74	8. 3)129	9. 6)363
10. 27)91	11. 64)776	12. 26)78	13. 14)580

Complete.

14. 3 feet = _____ yard

15. 9 feet = _____ yards

16. 12 yards = _____ feet

17. 96 inches = _____ feet

18. 144 inches = _____ yards

19. 12 feet = _____ inches

43

▷ Use two steps to solve.

	Step 1	Step 2
20. Ms. Bing collected 241 eggs from the hen house. She sold 133 eggs to a nearby store. She put the remaining eggs into egg cartons with 12 sections each. How many full egg cartons did she have then?		cartons
21. Michael bought 21 yards of material to make curtains for 3 windows. How many yards of material will he need to make curtains for 8 windows that are the same size?		yards
22. Lauren put 98 apples in each basket. She had 5 baskets filled with apples. She sold 346 apples in one day. How many apples did Lauren have left?		apples
23. Teng drove 136 miles in the morning. She drove 178 miles in the afternoon. She will drive this far each day for 5 days. How far will Teng drive in 5 days?		miles
24. There were 325 nails in a box. Jim bought 3 boxes. He used 468 nails to build a tree house. How many nails did Jim have left?		nails

3 Adding and Subtracting Decimals

▼ ▼ ▼ ▼ ▼ ▼ ▼

Steven made a grid design on his computer. There were 1,000 squares on the design. He colored 342 of the squares red. Write a decimal to show what part of the grid was red.

Solve

▷ Write a problem to show another color Steven may have used.

Tenths and Hundredths

 The square is divided into 10 equal parts. Each part is 1 **tenth** of the square.

 When a square is divided into 100 equal parts, each part is called 1 **hundredth**.

A whole divided into tenths or hundredths can be written as a **decimal**. A **decimal point** is used to separate whole numbers from decimal parts.

5 tenths = 0.5
↑
decimal point

When a decimal is less than 1 whole, a **zero** is written before the decimal point.

2 and 35 hundredths = 2.35

In a decimal greater than 1, the decimal point is read as **and**:

2.35 = 2 and 35 hundredths

Guided Practice

▷Write each decimal.

1. 3 hundredths = _0.03_

2. 6 tenths = _____

3. 1 tenth = _____

4. 17 hundredths = _____

5. 9 and 2 tenths = _____

6. 24 and 8 hundredths = _____

7. 560 and 8 tenths = _____

8. 73 and 22 hundredths = _____

9. 10 and 3 hundredths = _____

10. 204 and 5 tenths = _____

Practice

▷ Write each decimal.

1. 7 tenths = _____

2. 9 tenths = _____

3. 2 tenths = _____

4. 4 tenths = _____

5. 1 hundredth = _____

6. 12 hundredths = _____

7. 55 hundredths = _____

8. 72 hundredths = _____

9. 1 and 3 tenths = _____

10. 6 and 8 tenths = _____

11. 29 and 1 tenth = _____

12. 48 and 5 tenths = _____

13. 3 and 25 hundredths = _____

14. 10 and 31 hundredths = _____

15. 42 and 6 hundredths = _____

16. 98 and 17 hundredths = _____

17. 100 and 52 hundredths = _____

18. 345 and 2 tenths = _____

19. 840 and 9 tenths = _____

20. 840 and 9 hundredths = _____

Using Math

▷ Here is a list of facts Yoshi wrote about herself. She left the decimal points out of the numbers. Write the correct decimal number after each fact.

I am 1375 years old. _____

My weight is 1105 pounds. _____

My height is 525 feet. _____

Thousandths

Study the place-value chart. It shows that as a digit moves to the right of the ones' place, its value becomes smaller.

hundreds	tens	ones	.	tenths	hundredths	thousandths	
	6	5	.	7			= 65.7 = 65 and 7 tenths
		6	.	5	7		= 6.57 = 6 and 57 hundredths
		0	.	6	5	7	= 0.657 = 657 thousandths

↑
decimal point

Write a zero when there are no ones, tenths, or hundredths.

4 tenths	= 0.4	←—— no ones
6 hundredths	= 0.06	←—— no ones, no tenths
8 thousandths	= 0.008	←—— no ones, no tenths, no hundredths

Guided Practice

▷Write each decimal.

1. 4 and 2 thousandths = __4.002__

2. 525 thousandths = _____

3. 36 thousandths = _____

4. 94 and 6 thousandths = _____

5. 17 and 3 thousandths = _____

6. 841 thousandths = _____

▷Complete.

7. 0.472 = __472__ thousandths

8. 0.016 = _____ thousandths

9. 3.094 = _____ and _____ thousandths

10. 28.005 = _____ and _____ thousandths

11. 0.519 = _____ thousandths

12. 44.013 = _____ and _____ thousandths

Practice

▷ Write each decimal.

1. 3 tenths = _____

2. 17 hundredths = _____

3. 64 thousandths = _____

4. 5 and 8 tenths = _____

5. 2 hundredths = _____

6. 19 and 5 thousandths = _____

7. 77 and 9 hundredths = _____

8. 1 and 1 tenth = _____

9. 250 and 75 hundredths = _____

10. 600 and 756 thousandths = _____

▷ Complete.

11. 0.15 = _____ hundredths

12. 0.711 = _____ thousandths

13. 0.9 = _____ tenths

14. 0.024 = _____ thousandths

15. 6.05 = _____ and _____ hundredths

16. 3.8 = _____ and _____ tenths

17. 40.007 = _____ and _____ thousandths

18. 92.42 = _____ and _____ hundredths

19. 189.9 = _____ and _____ tenths

20. 544.015 = _____ and _____ thousandths

Using Math

▷ Frank read that the smallest spider in the world measures 16 thousandths of an inch. Write the number for the size of the spider.

_____ of an inch

Comparing Decimals

Compare the shaded parts of these examples.

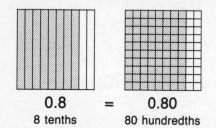

0.8   =   0.80
8 tenths   80 hundredths

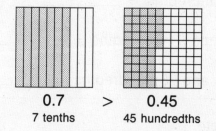

0.7   >   0.45
7 tenths   45 hundredths

To compare decimals, first line up the decimal points. Then start at the left and compare digits that are in the same place.

6.387
6.324

Step 1   Compare the ones. 6 ones and 6 ones are the same, so compare the next digit.

Step 2   Compare the tenths. 3 tenths and 3 tenths are the same, so compare the next digit.

Step 3   Compare the hundredths. 8 hundredths is greater than 2 hundredths, so 6.387 > 6.324.

Guided Practice

▷ Compare the decimals. Write >, <, or =.

1. 1.6 __>__ 1.06

2. 0.71 _____ 0.83

3. 1.659 _____ 1.65

4. 2.7 _____ 2.70

5. 5.17 _____ 5.3

6. 1 _____ 0.99

7. 4.05 _____ 4.15

8. 34.2 _____ 34.02

9. 0.060 _____ 0.06

10. 85.11 _____ 85.12

11. 2.7 _____ 2.07

12. 0.91 _____ 0.913

50

Practice

▷ Compare the decimals. Write >, <, or = .

1. 0.4 _____ 0.3

2. 0.69 _____ 0.96

3. 10.7 _____ 10.9

4. 0.582 _____ 0.585

5. 0.3 _____ 0.30

6. 1.04 _____ 1.02

7. 2.86 _____ 2.85

8. 0.92 _____ 0.920

9. 5.881 _____ 5.896

10. 0.1 _____ 0.01

11. 1.33 _____ 1.336

12. 4.54 _____ 4.540

13. 1.95 _____ 1.905

14. 0.86 _____ 1

15. 7.255 _____ 7.258

16. 0.007 _____ 0.07

17. 3.642 _____ 3.639

18. 9 _____ 9.00

19. 28.75 _____ 28.749

20. 73.4 _____ 73.40

21. 0.84 _____ 1

22. 14.091 _____ 14.18

23. 6.000 _____ 6

24. 0.954 _____ 0.944

Using Math

▷ Maria has 4 dollar bills and 52 pennies. Manuel has 4 dollar
bills and 6 dimes. Does Maria have more or less money
than Manuel? Write each amount of money as a decimal.
Then circle the correct symbol.

Work here.

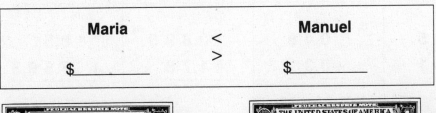

Maria		Manuel
	<	
	>	
$_____		$_____

51

Adding Decimals

When you add decimals, line up the decimal points. Then add as you would whole numbers. Begin adding with the digits at the right.

Sometimes when you add decimals you need to write zeros to hold places. Writing a zero after the last digit does not change the value of the decimal.

$$
\begin{array}{r}
0.1\,5 \\
+0.8\,3 \\
\hline
0.9\,8 \\
\end{array}
$$
←——•

Step 1 Line up the decimal points.	Step 2 Write a zero.	Step 3 Add.
$$\begin{array}{r} 7.9\,8 \\ +4.6 \\ \hline \end{array}$$	$$\begin{array}{r} 7.9\,8 \\ +4.6\,0 \\ \hline \end{array}$$	$$\begin{array}{r} \overset{1}{} \\ 7.9\,8 \\ +4.6\,0 \\ \hline 1\,2.5\,8 \\ \end{array}$$ Remember to write the decimal point in the answer.

Guided Practice

▷ Add. Write one or more zeros if needed.

1. $$\begin{array}{r} \overset{\text{l}}{} \\ 0.7 \\ +0.6 \\ \hline 1.3 \\ \end{array}$$	2. $$\begin{array}{r} 3.9\,5 \\ +0.4\,1 \\ \hline \end{array}$$	3. $$\begin{array}{r} 0.4\,8 \\ +0.3 \\ \hline \end{array}$$	4. $$\begin{array}{r} 2.8\,9\,5 \\ +1.7\,8 \\ \hline \end{array}$$	5. $$\begin{array}{r} 1\,8.5 \\ +\quad 7.5\,9\,3 \\ \hline \end{array}$$
6. $$\begin{array}{r} 3.6\,5 \\ +4.1\,7\,2 \\ \hline \end{array}$$	7. $$\begin{array}{r} 2\,6.4\,3\,8 \\ +3\,5.3\,7 \\ \hline \end{array}$$	8. $$\begin{array}{r} 0.8 \\ +0.5\,7 \\ \hline \end{array}$$	9. $$\begin{array}{r} 4\,5.8 \\ +\quad 6.4\,9 \\ \hline \end{array}$$	10. $$\begin{array}{r} 2\,3\,3.9\,9 \\ +3\,8\,1.8 \\ \hline \end{array}$$

Practice

▷ Add. Write one or more zeros if needed.

1. 0.3 +0.4	2. 0.8 +0.7	3. 1.7 +5.9	4. 6.6 2 +0.3 8	5. 0.4 1 7 +0.6 5 1
6. 7 2.6 +3 6.7	7. 5 5.7 +4 4.3	8. 1 2.8 5 + 6.0 3	9. 3.2 9 9 +6.4 5 9	10. 2 6.1 8 + 8.8 5
11. 1 7.8 6 1 +1 1.1 5 9	12. 0.1 7 5 +0.3 8	13. 6 2.1 + 8.5 8	14. 4.2 5 +0.9	15. 3.2 9 +5 6.5 1
16. 6 3.0 9 9 + 3.9 0 1	17. 2.4 8 +0.6 1 4	18. 9.8 +0.7 6 2	19. 1 8 6.4 5 +4 8 9.5	20. 8 6.9 4 +1 5 9.2

Problem Solving

▷ Use two steps to solve.

Maria bought 2 pounds of bananas for $.64 in all. How much would 3 pounds of bananas cost?

Step 1	Step 2
	in all

Subtracting Decimals

When you subtract decimals, line up the decimal points. Then subtract as you would whole numbers. Begin subtracting with the digits at the right.

$$\begin{array}{r} 0.7\,8 \\ -\,0.6\,4 \\ \hline 0.1\,4 \end{array}$$

Sometimes you need to change a whole number to a decimal before you can subtract. To change a whole number to a decimal, write a decimal point after the ones' digit. Then write one or more zeros after the decimal point.

Subtract $1.25 from $8.

Step 1 Write a decimal point after the ones' digit.	**Step 2** Write 2 zeros after the decimal point.	**Step 3** Subtract.
$ 8. − 1.2 5	$ 8.0 0 − 1.2 5	9 7 1̷ 10 $ 8̷.0̷ 0̷ − 1.2 5 $ 6.7 5

Guided Practice

▷ Subtract. Write one or more zeros if needed.

1. ⁶ ¹⁰ 0.7 0̷ − 0.6 6 0.04	2. ³ ¹⁰ 4̷.0̷ − 2.3 1.7	3. 2.0 6 − 1.8 4	4. 8.7 5 9 − 0.6	5. 1 5.4 6 − 8.2
6. 4.4 − 1.7	7. 0.6 1 5 − 0.0 7 9	8. 2.3 7 5 − 1.2 8 7	9. 6 − 3.1 9	10. 6 2.2 4 9 − 5.3 8

Practice

▷ Subtract. Write one or more zeros if needed.

1. $\begin{array}{r} 0.9 \\ -\,0.5 \\ \hline \end{array}$	2. $\begin{array}{r} 3.6 \\ -\,2.8 \\ \hline \end{array}$	3. $\begin{array}{r} 1.1\,7 \\ -\,0.4\,3 \\ \hline \end{array}$	4. $\begin{array}{r} 0.5\,0\,8 \\ -\,0.1\,2\,4 \\ \hline \end{array}$	5. $\begin{array}{r} 6.3\,1 \\ -\,4.0\,9 \\ \hline \end{array}$
6. $\begin{array}{r} 9.1\,5\,6 \\ -\,3.2\,8\,5 \\ \hline \end{array}$	7. $\begin{array}{r} 1\,2.4 \\ -\ \ 6.7 \\ \hline \end{array}$	8. $\begin{array}{r} 3\,8.4\,2 \\ -\,3\,7.6\,2 \\ \hline \end{array}$	9. $\begin{array}{r} 2.1\,7 \\ -\,2.1 \\ \hline \end{array}$	10. $\begin{array}{r} 5.6 \\ -\,0.9\,8 \\ \hline \end{array}$
11. $\begin{array}{r} 0.0\,3\,6 \\ -\,0.0\,1 \\ \hline \end{array}$	12. $\begin{array}{r} 2\,9.1 \\ -\,1\,5.8\,5 \\ \hline \end{array}$	13. $\begin{array}{r} 7\,3.3\,5\,3 \\ -\ \ 4.4\,9 \\ \hline \end{array}$	14. $\begin{array}{r} 2.1\,9 \\ -\,0.7\,8\,6 \\ \hline \end{array}$	15. $\begin{array}{r} 1\,5\,6.8 \\ -\ \ \ 3.6\,1 \\ \hline \end{array}$
16. $\begin{array}{r} 2 \\ -\,1.5 \\ \hline \end{array}$	17. $\begin{array}{r} 8.7\,6 \\ -\,3 \\ \hline \end{array}$	18. $\begin{array}{r} 1.7 \\ -\,1 \\ \hline \end{array}$	19. $\begin{array}{r} 1\,4.9\,1 \\ -\,1\,2 \\ \hline \end{array}$	20. $\begin{array}{r} 1\,8\,2 \\ -\,1\,8\,1.9\,9 \\ \hline \end{array}$

Using Math

▷ Leslie received a coupon from a clothing store in the mail.
The coupon was for $3.00 off any purchase over $20.00.
The next day she went shopping. She bought a sweater
that had a price tag of $23.50. She showed the salesperson
the coupon. How much did she pay for the sweater?

Work here.

Leslie paid _____ for the sweater.

Rounding Decimals

Rounding decimals is like rounding whole numbers.

Round 16.8 to the nearest whole number.

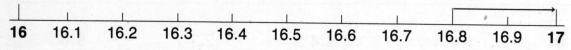

| 16 | 16.1 | 16.2 | 16.3 | 16.4 | 16.5 | 16.6 | 16.7 | 16.8 | 16.9 | 17 |

Since 16.8 is closer to 17 than 16, round up to 17.

Round 0.435 to the nearest tenth.

Step 1	Underline the place you are rounding to.	0.4 3 5
Step 2	Circle the next digit to the right.	0.4③5
Step 3	If the circled digit is less than 5, round down. If the circled digit is 5 or more, round up.	0.4

tenth

hundredth

Guided Practice

▷Round to the nearest whole number.

1. 0.92 __1__   2. 3.5 _____   3. 17.369 _____

4. 8.416 _____   5. 0.619 _____   6. 75.82 _____

▷Round each number to the nearest tenth.

7. 0.75 __0.8__   8. 1.818 _____   9. 42.06 _____

10. 17.26 _____   11. 3.644 _____   12. 95.22 _____

▷Round each number to the nearest hundredth.

13. 0.029 __0.03__   14. 5.587 _____   15. 83.515 _____

16. 77.865 _____   17. 0.431 _____   18. 6.008 _____

56

Practice

▷ Round to the nearest whole number.

1. 0.8 _____   2. 2.3 _____   3. 35.6 _____

4. 5.52 _____   5. 17.19 _____   6. 44.088 _____

▷ Round each number to the nearest tenth.

7. 0.47 _____   8. 6.12 _____   9. 52.87 _____

10. 0.105 _____   11. 2.091 _____   12. 13.636 _____

▷ Round each number to the nearest hundredth.

13. 0.248 _____   14. 0.955 _____   15. 7.007 _____

16. 4.121 _____   17. 59.062 _____   18. 28.966 _____

Using Math

▷ Brian's mother asked him to buy 5 items at the store. She gave him $6.50. Did Brian have enough money to buy everything on the list? Round the cost of each item to the nearest dollar to find the answer.

Work here.

Brian _____ have enough money.
      did   did not

$1.89 $0.79 $1.99 $1.39 $1.09

Centimeters, Meters, and Kilometers

Short lengths can be measured in **metric** units called **centimeters**.
The width of your finger is about 1 centimeter.

Longer lengths are measured in units called **meters**.
The length of a desktop is about 1 meter long.

Kilometers are used to measure much longer lengths or distances.
It takes about 10 minutes to walk about 1 kilometer.

100 centimeters = 1 meter	1,000 meters = 1 kilometer

To change lengths to a smaller unit, such as meters to centimeters, multiply.	To change lengths to a larger unit, such as meters to kilometers, divide.
3 meters = <u> ? </u> centimeters 3 × <u>100</u> = 300 centimeters 100 centimeters = 1 meter	3,000 meters = <u> ? </u> kilometers 3,000 ÷ <u>1,000</u> = 3 kilometers 1,000 meters = 1 kilometer

Guided Practice

▷ Ring the unit of measure you would use.

1. a chalkboard (meter) kilometer	2. a car trip centimeter kilometer	3. a pencil centimeter meter

▷ Complete.

4. 200 centimeters = <u> 2 </u> meters

5. 2,000 meters = _____ kilometers

6. 4 meters = _____ centimeters

7. 15 kilometers = _____ meters

58

Practice

▷ Ring the best length or distance.

1. length of a soccer field
 	
     100 meters   100 kilometers
	2. length of a ballpoint pen
	
	     16 centimeters 16 meters

3. distance from Orlando to Miami
 	
     142 meters   142 kilometers
	4. length of a classroom
	
	     10 centimeters 10 meters

▷ Complete.

5. 800 centimeters = _____ meters

6. 6 meters = _____ centimeters

7. 3,000 meters = _____ kilometers

8. 12 kilometers = _____ meters

9. 52 meters = _____ centimeters

10. 7,000 meters = _____ kilometers

11. 24,000 meters = _____ kilometers

12. 3,600 centimeters = _____ meters

13. 4 kilometers = _____ meters

14. 15,000 meters = _____ kilometers

15. 300 centimeters = _____ meters

16. 20 kilometers = _____ meters

17. 86 meters = _____ centimeters

18. 10,000 meters = _____ kilometers

19. 75,000 meters = _____ kilometers

20. 400 centimeters = _____ meters

Using Math

▷ Melissa practices running on a 200-meter track. In one week, she ran around the track 45 times. How many kilometers did she run?

Work here.

Melissa ran _____ kilometers.

Problem Solving

Estimation

22,645 people live in Fairbanks, Alaska.

19,528 people live in Juneau, Alaska.

About how many people in all live in these two cities?

> The word **about** means an exact answer is not needed.
> You can estimate the answer.

▷ Round each number to the nearest thousand.

| Step 1 | Underline the place you are rounding to. | 2 2 , 6 4 5 |
| | | 1 9 , 5 2 8 |

| Step 2 | Circle the next digit to the right. | 2 2 , ⑥ 4 5 |
| | | 1 9 , ⑤ 2 8 |

Step 3 If the circled digit is less than 5, round down.

If the circled digit is 5 or more, round up.

$$2\,2,\textcircled{6}4\,5 \longrightarrow 23,000$$
$$\underline{+1\,9,\textcircled{5}2\,8} \longrightarrow \underline{+ 20,000}$$

There are about 43,000 people in both cities.

Guided Practice

▷ Round to the nearest thousand.
Estimate to solve.

The land area of Kuwait is
6,880 square miles. The state of
Delaware has about 2,044 square miles
of land. About how many more
square miles of land does Kuwait
have than Delaware?

6,880 ⟶ _____

−2,044 ⟶ _____

▮▮▮▮▮ about _____ square miles

60

Practice

▶ Round to the nearest thousand.
Estimate to solve.

1. Dana Valdez and Nelson Brown led two groups of mountain climbers last summer. Dana's group climbed 2,810 feet. Nelson's group climbed 2,080 feet. About how much higher did Dana's group climb than Nelson's group climbed?

$$2,810 \longrightarrow$$
$$-\,2,080 \longrightarrow$$

about _____ feet

2. Mount McKinley has two peaks. The North Peak is 19,470 feet above sea level. The South Peak is 20,320 feet high. About how much higher is the South Peak than the North Peak?

$$20,320 \longrightarrow$$
$$-\,19,470 \longrightarrow$$

about _____ feet

3. By the end of the 1989 football season, Joe Montana had completed 2,593 career passes. Fran Tarkenton's career total was 3,686 passes that year. About how many more passes did Tarkenton complete than Montana?

$$3,686 \longrightarrow$$
$$-\,2,593 \longrightarrow$$

about _____ passes

4. A library in Leander, Texas, has about 1,800 fiction books. The library has about the same number of nonfiction books. About how many books in all does this library have?

$$1,800 \longrightarrow$$
$$+\,1,800 \longrightarrow$$

about _____ books

Write each decimal. pages 46–47

1. 5 tenths = _____

2. 1 and 9 tenths = _____

3. 2 hundredths = _____

4. 6 and 15 hundredths = _____

5. 8 and 7 tenths = _____

6. 308 and 18 hundredths = _____

pages 48–49

7. 268 thousandths = _____

8. 71 thousandths = _____

9. 4 and 6 thousandths = _____

10. 15 and 802 thousandths = _____

11. 99 and 25 thousandths = _____

12. 312 and 4 thousandths = _____

Compare. Write >, <, or =. pages 50–51

13. 0.3 _____ 0.4

14. 3.9 _____ 3.8

15. 0.42 _____ 0.44

16. 6.7 _____ 6.70

17. 5.045 _____ 5.04

18. 8.635 _____ 8.653

19. 0.219 _____ 0.225

20. 11.300 _____ 11.3

21. 27.146 _____ 27.05

Add. Write one or more zeros if needed. pages 52–53

22.	23.	24.	25.	26.
0.4 +0.3	1.6 +0.7	1.48 +1.55	3.75 +2.95	0.972 +0.951
27.	28.	29.	30.	31.
2.4 +0.59	7.86 +0.4	6.5 +2.77	11.6 +9.674	9.069 +0.2

▷Subtract. Write one or more zeros if needed.   pages 54–55

32.	33.	34.	35.	36.
0.9 − 0.2	1.4 − 1.3	2.6 1 − 0.7 4	0.4 8 2 − 0.3 9 9	2.4 8 1 − 1.9 3 2
37.	38.	39.	40.	41.
4.8 2 − 1.6	0.6 − 0.4 2	2.4 − 1.8 9	0.9 − 0.7 3 6	5 − 1.6 5

▷Round to the nearest whole number.   pages 56–57

42. 0.8 _____

43. 4.36 _____

44. 22.592 _____

45. 55.156 _____

46. 0.9 _____

47. 7.83 _____

▷Round each number to the nearest tenth.

48. 0.61 _____

49. 2.55 _____

50. 19.727 _____

51. 43.718 _____

52. 0.361 _____

53. 5.48 _____

▷Round each number to the nearest hundredth.

54. 0.588 _____

55. 4.015 _____

56. 9.309 _____

57. 35.016 _____

58. 0.611 _____

59. 77.128 _____

▷Complete.   pages 58–59

60. 1 meter = _____ centimeters

61. 500 centimeters = _____ meters

62. 1,000 meters = _____ kilometer

63. 8 kilometers = _____ meters

64. 7 meters = _____ centimeters

65. 12,000 meters = _____ kilometers

Round to the nearest thousand.

Estimate to solve.

pages 60–61

66. There were 1,871 people at a music convention. 1,105 people left on Friday. Everyone else stayed until Saturday. About how many people stayed at the music convention until Saturday?

$1,871 \longrightarrow$ _____

$- 1,105 \longrightarrow$ _____

■ about _____ people

67. The peak at Mount Rainier is 4,392 meters above sea level. Mount Hood is 3,426 meters high. About how much higher is Mount Rainier than Mount Hood?

$4,392 \longrightarrow$ _____

$- 3,426 \longrightarrow$ _____

■ about _____ meters

68. Alaska has 5,580 miles of coastline along the Pacific Ocean. It has 1,060 miles of coastline along the Arctic Ocean. About how many miles of ocean coastline in all does Alaska have?

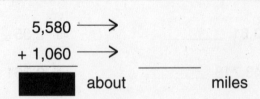

$5,580 \longrightarrow$ _____

$+ 1,060 \longrightarrow$ _____

■ about _____ miles

69. A railroad has 2,800 miles of track. If the company buys 1,246 more miles of track, about how many miles of track in all will they have?

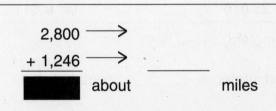

$2,800 \longrightarrow$ _____

$+ 1,246 \longrightarrow$ _____

■ about _____ miles

Write each decimal.

1. 59 hundredths = _____

2. 4 and 72 thousandths = _____

Compare. Write >, <, or =.

3. 0.7 _____ 0.9   4. 4.672 _____ 4.652   5. 0.8 _____ 0.80

Add. Write one or more zeros if needed.

6.	7.	8.	9.	10.
0.5	3.7 6	4.8	1.5 6	1 2.3 6 4
+0.4	+2.1 5	+0.6 7	+1.9	+ 2.8

Subtract. Write one or more zeros if needed.

11.	12.	13.	14.	15.
0.8	1.4 6	5.8 6 3	4.7	6
−0.5	−0.5 8	−1.9 6	−0.4 2	−3.7 5

Round to the nearest place.

16. **whole number**	17. **tenth**	18. **hundredth**
1.9 _____	0.63 _____	4.075 _____

Complete.

19. 100 centimeters = _____ meter

20. 7 meters = _____ centimeters

21. 5,000 meters = _____ kilometers

22. 4 kilometers = _____ meters

▷ Round to the nearest thousand.
Estimate to solve.

23. In 1980, Rayville, Louisiana, had
a population of 4,610 people. Vivian,   4,610 ⟶
Louisiana, had a population of 4,225 people.   + 4,225 ⟶ _____
About how many people in all lived   ■■■■ about   people
in Rayville and Vivian in 1980?

24. Last spring, Otto made a canoe trip   1,885 ⟶
that was 1,885 miles long. In the   + 2,315 ⟶ _____
summer, he went 2,315 miles in   ■■■■ about   miles
his canoe. About how many miles
in all were Otto's canoe trips?

25. Ms. Hernandez had 3,251 acres
of land. She bought 1,746 more acres   3,251 ⟶
of land yesterday. About how many   + 1,746 ⟶ _____
acres of land in all does Ms. Hernandez   ■■■■ about   acres
have now?

26. There were 6,925 people who
went to the county fair one year. The   6,925 ⟶
next year, 5,471 people went   − 5,471 ⟶ _____
to the county fair. About how many   ■■■■ about   people
more people went to the county
fair the first year than the next year?

CHAPTER 1

Cumulative Review

▷ Write the value of each underlined digit. pages 2–3

1. 4 7 <u>6</u>,9 3 5 _____

2. <u>3</u> 9 4,0 0 0 _____

3. <u>4</u>,3 0 7,2 9 5 _____

4. 9,6 <u>8</u> 2,7 5 0 _____

▷ Write each number. pages 2–3

5. 67 thousand, 901 _____

6. 2 million, 375 thousand, 81 _____

▷ Add. pages 4–7

7. $\begin{array}{r} 7\,3\,9 \\ +1\,8\,6 \end{array}$	8. $\begin{array}{r} 2{,}7\,8\,1 \\ +6{,}9\,4\,8 \end{array}$	9. $\begin{array}{r} 3\,6{,}8\,4\,0 \\ +4\,2{,}7\,6\,0 \end{array}$	10. $\begin{array}{r} 3\,9\,7{,}2\,8\,4 \\ +\ \ 6\,2{,}9\,6\,8 \end{array}$

▷ Subtract. pages 8–11

11. $\begin{array}{r} 5\,3\,7 \\ -1\,8\,6 \end{array}$	12. $\begin{array}{r} 5{,}9\,7\,6 \\ -2{,}1\,8\,9 \end{array}$	13. $\begin{array}{r} 8{,}0\,0\,0 \\ -2{,}6\,7\,4 \end{array}$	14. $\begin{array}{r} 8\,0{,}0\,0\,9 \\ -4\,7{,}6\,2\,5 \end{array}$

▷ Estimate each sum or difference by rounding the numbers to the place shown.

pages 12–13

15. **Nearest Hundred**	16. **Nearest Thousand**
$\begin{array}{r} 5{,}6\,3\,7 \longrightarrow \\ +2{,}8\,5\,1 \longrightarrow \end{array}$ + _____	$\begin{array}{r} 7\,4{,}7\,1\,7 \longrightarrow \\ -1\,6{,}4\,5\,0 \longrightarrow \end{array}$ – _____

▷ Circle the correct temperature. pages 14–15

17. The bath water is comfortable.	18. Ice cream melts.
20°F 85°F 210°F	10°F 30°F 50°F

▷ Multiply.   pages 24–27

1. $\begin{array}{r} 23 \\ \times\ 2 \\ \hline \end{array}$	2. $\begin{array}{r} 67 \\ \times 40 \\ \hline \end{array}$	3. $\begin{array}{r} 28 \\ \times 15 \\ \hline \end{array}$	4. $\begin{array}{r} 97 \\ \times 46 \\ \hline \end{array}$	5. $\begin{array}{r} 417 \\ \times\ 38 \\ \hline \end{array}$

▷ Divide.   pages 28–33

6. $3\overline{)69}$	7. $6\overline{)79}$	8. $4\overline{)168}$	9. $7\overline{)565}$
10. $19\overline{)78}$	11. $57\overline{)918}$	12. $25\overline{)75}$	13. $13\overline{)735}$

▷ Complete.   pages 36–37

14. 36 inches = _____ feet

15. 15,840 feet = _____ miles

16. 24 feet = _____ yards

17. 8 yards = _____ inches

18. 3 yards = _____ feet

19. 360 inches = _____ yards

68

▷ Write each decimal. pages 46–49

1. 78 hundredths = _____   2. 5 and 83 thousandths = _____

▷ Compare. Write >, <, or = . pages 50–51

3. 0.6 _____ 0.8   4. 3.981 _____ 3.976   5. 0.4 _____ 0.40

▷ Add. Write one or more zeros if needed. pages 52–53

6.	7.	8.	9.	10.
0.3 + 0.6	4.8 6 + 3.2 5	6.9 + 0.8 3	1.7 9 + 1.6	1 3.6 3 4 + 3.7

▷ Subtract. Write one or more zeros if needed. pages 54–55

11.	12.	13.	14.	15.
0.7 − 0.2	6.7 5 − 0.8 7	4.9 5 2 − 1.8 5	3.9 − 0.6 5	8 − 4.2 5

▷ Round to the nearest place. pages 56–57

16. **whole number**	17. **tenth**	18. **hundredth**
2.7 _____	0.72 _____	6.085 _____

▷ Complete. pages 58–59

19. 100 centimeters = _____ meter   20. 6,000 meters = _____ kilometers

21. 300 meters = _____ centimeters   22. 75 kilometers = _____ meters

▶ Use two steps to solve.

pages 16–17

	Step 1	Step 2
23. James had $587. He spent $120 on new tires and $65 on a new jacket. How much money did James have left?		left

pages 38–39

	Step 1	Step 2
24. The Czech Cafe sold 2 kolaches each to 70 people. They also sold 24 kolaches to Ms. Brown for a party. How many kolaches in all did they sell?		kolaches

▶ Round to the nearest thousand.

Estimate to solve.

pages 60–61

25. Mount Saint Helens is now 8,364 feet above sea level. In 1980, this volcano erupted and blew off about 1,000 feet of its height. How high was Mount Saint Helens in 1979?	8,364 ⟶ + 1,000 ⟶ ■ about ____ feet
26. Mr. Weiss bought a computer for $2,846. He bought a printer for $1,325. About how much did Mr. Weiss spend altogether?	$2,846 ⟶ + 1,325 ⟶ ■ about ____

4 Multiplying and Dividing Decimals

▼ ▼ ▼ ▼ ▼ ▼ ▼

April made a model that was 18.4 cm long and 16.2 cm wide. Then she made one that was twice as long and twice as wide. How long and wide was the second model?

Solve

Write your own problem about a model you might build.

Multiplying Decimals by Whole Numbers

Multiplying decimals is like multiplying whole numbers. First multiply the numbers. Then place the decimal point in the product.

Step 1 Multiply to find the product.	**Step 2** Count the number of decimal places in the factors.	**Step 3** Place the decimal point in the product.

Step 1

```
      1 1
    2.3 4
  ×   3 2
    4 6 8  ← 2 × 234
 + 7 0 2 0 ← 30 × 234
   7 4 8 8
```

Step 2

```
    2.3 4 ── 2 decimal places
  ×   3 2    0 decimal places
    4 6 8
 + 7 0 2 0
   7 4 8 8
```

Step 3

```
    2.3 4 ── 2 decimal places
  ×   3 2    0 decimal places
    4 6 8
 + 7 0 2 0
   7 4.8 8 ── 2 decimal places
```

> The number of decimal places in the product is the same as the number of decimal places in the factors.

Guided Practice

▷ Multiply.

1.	2.	3.	4.	5.
$$\begin{array}{r} \overset{2}{0.1\,6} \\ \times\ \ \ \ 4 \\ \hline 0.64 \end{array}$$	$$\begin{array}{r} 1.6\,1\,5 \\ \times\ \ \ \ \ 5 \\ \hline \end{array}$$	$$\begin{array}{r} 0.0\,9 \\ \times\ \ 1\,5 \\ \hline \end{array}$$	$$\begin{array}{r} 1\,7\,6.1\,8 \\ \times\ \ \ \ \ \ 2 \\ \hline \end{array}$$	$$\begin{array}{r} 5.0\,6 \\ \times\ \ 6\,7 \\ \hline \end{array}$$

Practice

▷ Multiply.

1. $\begin{array}{r} 0.2 \\ \times\ \ 3 \\ \hline \end{array}$	2. $\begin{array}{r} 2.6\,2 \\ \times\ \ 3\,4 \\ \hline \end{array}$	3. $\begin{array}{r} 0.2\,1 \\ \times\ \ \ \ 4 \\ \hline \end{array}$	4. $\begin{array}{r} 1.0\,7\,1 \\ \times\ \ \ \ 5\,6 \\ \hline \end{array}$	5. $\begin{array}{r} 0.3\,0\,5 \\ \times\ \ \ \ \ 9 \\ \hline \end{array}$
6. $\begin{array}{r} 7.4 \\ \times\ \ 8 \\ \hline \end{array}$	7. $\begin{array}{r} 1\,5.0\,6 \\ \times\ \ \ \ \ 2 \\ \hline \end{array}$	8. $\begin{array}{r} 2.5\,3 \\ \times\ \ \ 2\,3 \\ \hline \end{array}$	9. $\begin{array}{r} 0.7\,8 \\ \times\ \ \ 3\,8 \\ \hline \end{array}$	10. $\begin{array}{r} 1\,5\,5.2\,3 \\ \times\ \ \ \ \ \ 5 \\ \hline \end{array}$
11. $\begin{array}{r} 0.3 \\ \times 1\,1 \\ \hline \end{array}$	12. $\begin{array}{r} 0.0\,5 \\ \times\ \ 2\,5 \\ \hline \end{array}$	13. $\begin{array}{r} 0.9\,6 \\ \times\ \ 1\,3 \\ \hline \end{array}$	14. $\begin{array}{r} 1.7\,8\,2 \\ \times\ \ \ \ \ 4 \\ \hline \end{array}$	15. $\begin{array}{r} 0.9\,0\,2 \\ \times\ \ \ \ 7\,4 \\ \hline \end{array}$

Using Math

▷ The students in the school play wanted to buy their drama
teacher a gift. They saw a book that cost $15.50. The tax
was $0.75. If each of the 11 students donated $1.50, would
they have enough money to buy the book? Circle your
answer. Then write how much money the students would
collect.

Work here.

Yes   No   They would collect _____.

73

Multiplying Tenths and Hundredths

When you multiply two decimals, first multiply the numbers. Then place the decimal point in the product. The sum of the decimal places in both factors is used to place the decimal point in the product.

$$
\begin{array}{r}
2\ 2 \\
6.4\,4 \\
\times\ \ 2.5 \\
\hline
3\ 2\ 2\ 0 \\
1\ 2\ 8\ 8\ 0 \\
\hline
1\ 6.1\,0\,0
\end{array}
$$

6.44 —— 2 decimal places

× 2.5 —— +1 decimal place

16.100 —— 3 decimal places

Drop the zeros. 16.100 = 16.1

> If the last digits in a decimal are zeros, drop them. Dropping the last zeros in a decimal does not change the value of the number.

Guided Practice

▷ Multiply.

1. ⁴ 0.6 ×0.8 0.48	2. 3.9 ×0.9	3. 3.5 6 × 4.1	4. 1 7.5 × 2.8	5. 3.7 2 × 6.5

Practice

Multiply.

1. 0.6 × 0.2	2. 0.8 × 0.5	3. 1.7 × 0.8	4. 1.2 7 × 0.4	5. 3.0 5 × 0.6
6. 6 5.1 × 0.7	7. 2.4 × 1.5	8. 4.8 × 2.1	9. 1.6 3 × 7.6	10. 7.2 × 5.7
11. 9 6.1 × 2.9	12. 7.1 5 × 3.8	13. 1 6.1 × 4.6	14. 8 5.2 × 2.5	15. 2 3.8 × 0.5 5

Using Math

It takes Emma 1.7 minutes to run one lap around the school track. How many minutes does it take her to run 5.5 laps?

Work here.

It takes her _____ minutes to run 5.5 laps.

75

Zeros in the Product

Sometimes you need to write one or more zeros in the product before placing the decimal point.

0.2 1 decimal place **× 3** **0.6** 1 decimal place └── Write a zero before the decimal point if the decimal is less than 1.	**0.2** 1 decimal place **×0.3** +1 decimal place **0.0 6** 2 decimal places └── Write one zero in the product so you have 2 decimal places.	**0.0 2** 2 decimal places **× 0.3** +1 decimal place **0.0 0 6** 3 decimal places └─ Write two zeros in the product so you have 3 decimal places.

Guided Practice

▷ Multiply.

1. **0.3** **×0.3** *0.09*	2. **0.0 1** **× 0.6**	3. **0.1 9** **× 0.4**	4. **2.1** **×0.0 3**	5. **0.0 2** **× 0.5**
6. **4.3** **×0.0 2**	7. **0.0 5** **× 0.5**	8. **0.1 1** **× 0.9**	9. **1.6** **×0.0 3**	10. **0.0 7** **× 0.4**

Practice

▷ Multiply.

1. 0.8 × 0.1	2. 0.0 2 × 0.7	3. 0.2 × 0.2	4. 0.0 9 × 0.8	5. 0.0 1 × 0.4
6. 1.6 × 0.0 3	7. 0.0 7 × 0.5	8. 0.0 4 × 0.2	9. 0.1 4 × 0.7	10. 2.4 × 0.0 2
11. 0.0 2 × 0.3	12. 0.1 × 0.1	13. 4.3 × 0.0 2	14. 0.7 × 0.0 1	15. 0.0 4 × 0.5
16. 0.0 6 × 0.6	17. 0.2 5 × 0.3	18. 0.1 6 × 0.5	19. 0.4 9 × 0.2	20. 2.2 × 0.0 3

Using Math

▷ A fast-moving snail can travel 0.03 mile in one hour. How far can this snail travel in 1.5 hours?

Work here.

The snail can travel _____ mile in 1.5 hours.

Dividing Decimals by Whole Numbers

Dividing decimals by whole numbers is like dividing whole numbers.

Step 1 Write the decimal point in the quotient directly above the decimal point in the dividend. $5\overline{)10.15}$	**Step 2** Divide as you would with whole numbers. $\begin{array}{r} 2.03 \\ 5\overline{)10.15} \\ -10 \\ \hline 01 \\ -0 \\ \hline 15 \\ -15 \\ \hline 0 \end{array}$

Guided Practice

▷ Divide.

1. $\begin{array}{r} 2.31 \\ 3\overline{)6.93} \\ -6 \\ \hline 09 \\ -9 \\ \hline 03 \\ -3 \\ \hline 0 \end{array}$	2. $7\overline{)3.71}$	3. $5\overline{)16.5}$	4. $2\overline{)4.184}$
5. $7\overline{)19.6}$	6. $3\overline{)1.83}$	7. $1\overline{)18.6}$	8. $4\overline{)18.8}$

78

Practice

▷ Divide.

1. $4\overline{)8.4}$	2. $6\overline{)1.9\ 8}$	3. $8\overline{)0.9\ 3\ 6}$	4. $2\overline{)7.5\ 8}$
5. $6\overline{)3.6\ 9\ 6}$	6. $7\overline{)4\ 9.4\ 2}$	7. $3\overline{)2.9\ 3\ 4}$	8. $5\overline{)3\ 0.2\ 5}$
9. $3\overline{)1.8\ 9}$	10. $5\overline{)2\ 0.6\ 7\ 5}$	11. $8\overline{)1\ 6.4\ 8}$	12. $4\overline{)2\ 1.6\ 8}$

Problem Solving

▷ Round to the nearest thousand.

Estimate to solve.

There were 2,789 people who visited the art museum in June. 2,341 visited the museum in July. About how many people visited the art museum during both months?

$2,789 \longrightarrow$ _____

$+\ 2,341 \longrightarrow +$ _____

▮ about _____ people

Writing Zeros in the Dividend

Sometimes you need to write one or more zeros in the dividend to complete the division.

Divide 3.5 by 14.

Step 1

Write the decimal point in the quotient. Divide until you have used each digit in the dividend.

```
      0.2
14)3.5
   -2 8
      7
```

Step 2

Write a zero after the last digit in the dividend. Complete the division.

```
      0.2 5
14)3.5 0
   -2 8
      7 0
     -7 0
        0
```

Guided Practice

▷ Divide.

1.
```
      0.35
16)5.60
   -48
     80
    -80
      0
```

2.
```
12)6 5.4
```

3.
```
15)6 8.4
```

4.
```
18)7 1.1
```

5.
```
14)1 3.3
```

6.
```
35)5 3.2
```

7.
```
88)9.2 4
```

8.
```
25)6 5.5
```

80

Practice

Divide.

1. $16\overline{)5.6}$	2. $14\overline{)25.9}$	3. $12\overline{)6.6}$	4. $15\overline{)37.2}$
5. $14\overline{)70.7}$	6. $12\overline{)84.6}$	7. $18\overline{)26.1}$	8. $20\overline{)6.08}$
9. $25\overline{)37.0}$	10. $18\overline{)13.5}$	11. $32\overline{)84.8}$	12. $16\overline{)15.2}$

Using Math

Juan and his father are going on an overnight biking trip. They will be traveling 85.8 miles in 12 hours. How many miles will they travel each hour if they ride at a steady speed?

They will travel _____ miles each hour.

Dividing by Tenths and Hundredths

When dividing by tenths and hundredths, change the divisor to a whole number.

<table>
<tr><td>

When dividing by tenths, multiply the divisor and the dividend by 10. Write the decimal point in the quotient and divide.

</td><td>

```
      0.5
0.7)0.3 5
    -3 5
       0
```

</td><td>

When dividing by hundredths, multiply the divisor and the dividend by 100. Write the decimal point in the quotient and divide.

</td><td>

```
        2 1.8
0.0 2)0.4 3 6
      - 4
        0 3
        - 2
          1 6
         -1 6
             0
```

</td></tr>
</table>

Remember that multiplying a decimal by 10 moves the decimal point one place to the right. Multiplying a decimal by 100 moves the decimal point two places to the right.

Guided Practice

▷ Divide.

<table>
<tr><td>

1.
```
        0.8
0.8)0.6 4
    - 6 4
         0
```

</td><td>

2.
```
0.0 4)0.6 3 2
```

</td><td>

3.
```
0.6)3.6 6
```

</td><td>

4.
```
0.1 4)0.4 5 5
```

</td></tr>
</table>

82

Practice

▷ Divide.

1. $0.8\overline{)0.2\ 7\ 2}$	2. $0.0\ 2\overline{)0.7\ 6}$	3. $0.6\overline{)3.8\ 6\ 4}$	4. $0.0\ 3\overline{)7.1\ 9\ 4}$
5. $0.2\overline{)5.5\ 3\ 2}$	6. $0.1\ 7\overline{)1.1\ 0\ 5}$	7. $0.4\ 8\overline{)1\ 0.5\ 6}$	8. $0.5\overline{)1.2\ 1\ 5}$
9. $0.2\ 1\overline{)5.4\ 6}$	10. $0.4\ 2\overline{)2.4\ 7\ 8}$	11. $0.9\overline{)1\ 4.4}$	12. $0.3\ 7\overline{)5.0\ 3\ 2}$

Using Math

▷ The Science Club made $18.56 selling muffins at the bake
sale. Each muffin cost $0.29. How many muffins did the
Science Club sell?

Work here.

The Science Club sold _____ muffins.

Milliliters and Liters

Milliliters and **liters** are metric units that measure liquid **capacity**, or how much a container holds.

An eyedropper holds about 1 milliliter.
A carton of juice holds about 1 liter.

1,000 milliliters = 1 liter

To change a larger unit to a smaller unit, such as liters to milliliters, multiply.	To change a smaller unit to a larger unit, such as milliliters to liters, divide.
2.5 liters = __?__ milliliters 2.5 × 1000 = 2,500 milliliters 1,000 milliliters = 1 liter	375 milliliters = __?__ liters 375 ÷ 1,000 = 0.375 liters 1,000 milliliters = 1 liter

Guided Practice

▷Ring the unit of measure you would use.

1. juice in a cup 　　milliliter　　liter	2. gasoline in a car 　　milliliter　　liter

▷Complete.

3. 258 milliliters = _____ liter

4. 94 milliliters = _____ liters

5. 1,750 milliliters = _____ liter

6. 0.436 liter = _____ milliliters

7. 0.059 liter = _____ milliliters

8. 3.7 liters = _____ milliliters

Practice

▷ Ring the unit of measure you would use.

1. soup in a bowl
 	
    milliliter   liter
	2. water in a swimming pool
	
	    milliliter liter

3. water in a fish tank
 	
    milliliter   liter
	4. medicine in a spoon
	
	    milliliter liter

5. a large carton of milk
 	
    milliliter   liter
	6. perfume in a bottle
	
	    milliliter liter

▷ Complete.

7. 1 milliliter = _____ liter

8. 425 milliliters = _____ liter

9. 2 liters = _____ milliliters

10. 0.594 liter = _____ milliliters

11. 3.897 liters = _____ milliliters

12. 250 milliliters = _____ liter

13. 12.1 liters = _____ milliliters

14. 6.57 liters = _____ milliliters

15. 625 milliliters = _____ liter

16. 4.25 liters = _____ milliliters

17. 30.6 liters = _____ milliliters

18. 17 milliliters = _____ liter

19. 0.214 liter = _____ milliliters

20. 8 liters = _____ milliliters

Using Math

▷ Kathy helped Mrs. Sharpe put up signs in the store.
Someone forgot to put the decimal points on one sign.
Write the decimal points on the sign.

Large Bottle of Grape Juice
275 liters
$185

Problem Solving

Estimation

Ryan bought 3 bags of oranges. Each bag cost $1.89.

About how much money in all did Ryan spend?

> The word **about** means an exact answer is not needed.
> You can estimate the answer.

Rounding money is like rounding other numbers.

To round money to the nearest dollar, follow these steps.

Step 1	Underline the number in the ones place.	$1.89
Step 2	Circle the next digit to the right.	$1.⑧9
Step 3	If the circled digit is less than 5, round down.	

If the circled digit is 5 or more, round up.

$$\$1.⑧9 \longrightarrow \$2.00$$
$$\times \quad 3 \longrightarrow \times 3.00$$

Ryan spent about $6.00 on bags of oranges.

Guided Practice

▸ Round to the nearest dollar.

Estimate to solve.

---

1. The video store was selling videos for $15.23. Jan bought 7 videos. About how much money in all did Jan spend on videos?

$15.23 $\longrightarrow$ $ 15.00
× 7 $\longrightarrow$ × 7
        about $105.00

---

2. Andrea spent $5.59 on ice cream cones. She bought 6 cones. About how much did each cone cost?

6) $5.59 $\longrightarrow$ about $
           6) $

Practice

▷ Round to the nearest whole number.
Estimate to solve.

1. A can of paint costs $9.85.
   Mei bought 5 cans. About how
   much money in all did Mei spend?

   $9.85 ⟶
   × 5 ⟶ _____
   ▮▮▮▮ about

2. Margo bought 8 lobsters. She
   paid a total of $71.78 for
   them. About how much did
   each lobster cost?

   ▮▮▮▮ about
   8) $71.78 ⟶) _____

3. Axle got 3 pounds of dried
   chili peppers for $3.99 a pound.
   About how much money in all
   did Axle spend on peppers?

   $3.99 ⟶
   × 3 ⟶ _____
   ▮▮▮▮ about

4. Mr. Nguyen bought 4 yards of
   material. Each yard cost $11.98.
   About how much money in all
   did Mr. Nguyen spend?

   $11.98 ⟶
   × 4 ⟶ _____
   ▮▮▮▮ about

5. Ms. Burns bought 3 shirts
   for $48.22. About how much
   money did each shirt cost?

   ▮▮▮▮ about
   3) $48.22 ⟶) _____

6. Nicholas bought a gallon of
   milk for $1.97. About how
   much will it cost if Nicholas
   buys 2 gallons of milk?

   $1.97 ⟶
   × 2 ⟶ _____
   ▮▮▮▮ about

▷Multiply.

pages 72–73				
1. 0.7 × 6	2. 0.0 5 × 9	3. 1.0 1 9 × 8	4. 1.4 ×1 2	5. 0.3 5 × 3 7
6. 6.2 × 3	7. 0.5 8 1 × 7	8. 0.0 4 9 × 1 1	9. 2.6 4 × 4 8	10. 1 7.2 × 5 6

pages 74–75				
11. 0.9 ×0.3	12. 3.6 ×4.5	13. 7.4 2 × 6.8	14. 9 3.1 × 2.9	15. 8 5.2 ×0.7 5

pages 76–77				
16. 0.2 ×0.2	17. 0.0 4 × 0.5	18. 1.3 ×0.0 3	19. 0.0 3 × 0.2	20. 0.0 9 × 0.6

▷ Divide.

pages 78–79			
21. $3\overline{)2.9\ 1}$	22. $8\overline{)0.9\ 6\ 8}$	23. $4\overline{)9.4\ 8}$	24. $2\overline{)6.8\ 4}$
pages 80–81 25. $1\ 8\overline{)1\ 4.4}$	26. $1\ 5\overline{)1\ 3.8}$	27. $1\ 6\overline{)1\ 0.4}$	28. $1\ 4\overline{)4.9}$
pages 82–83 29. $0.5\overline{)0.4\ 6\ 5}$	30. $0.0\ 7\overline{)4.5\ 1\ 5}$	31. $0.9\overline{)5.2\ 2}$	32. $0.2\ 5\overline{)6.2\ 5}$

▷ **Complete.**   pages 84–85

33. 1,000 milliliters = _____ liter

34. 4,000 milliliters = _____ liters

35. 1 milliliter = _____ liter

36. 624 milliliters = _____ liter

37. 2.375 liters = _____ milliliters

38. 7.6 liters = _____ milliliters

▶Round to the nearest dollar.

Estimate to solve.

pages 86–87

39. A gallon of gas costs $1.23.
Ron put 9 gallons in his car.
About how much did Ron
pay for gas?

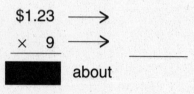

40. Ian had 4 boxes to mail. Postage
for each box cost $26.92. About how
much in all did Ian spend to mail
the boxes?

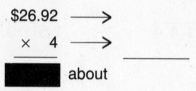

41. Angelo's family spent $19.85
on lunch. They bought 5 combo
meals. About how much did each
combo meal cost?

about

5) $19.85 ⟶)

42. A pound of coffee costs $6.99.
Doreen bought 2 pounds of coffee.
About how much did Doreen spend?

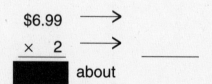

43. Tim spent $48.63 on shirts.
He bought 7 shirts that cost the
same price each. About how much
did each shirt cost?

about

7) $48.63 ⟶)

CHAPTER 4 **Test**

▷Multiply.

1. 0.4 2 × 2	2. 0.8 3 1 × 7	3. 5 6.1 × 0.7	4. 8.0 2 × 0.5	5. 2.8 9 × 0.3

6.
     1 7.3 1
 ×   2.2
	7.
	     3.0 4
	 × 2.5
		8.
		     1 9.8
		 × 6.8
			9.
			     0.0 2
			 × 0.4
				10.
				     0.0 8
				 × 0.6

▷Divide.

11. 6)8.4	12. 8)0.3 6	13. 2 0)5 0.2	14. 0.7)0.2 8
15. 1.9)8.9 3	16. 3.2)3 8.4	17. 0.0 2)0.1 5 8	18. 0.2 3)2.9 9

▷Complete.

19. 0.472 liter = _____ milliliters   20. 3,500 milliliters = _____ liters

91

▷Round to the nearest dollar.
Estimate to solve.

21. Joanna spent $17.53 on fabric.
    She will make 6 cushions for her
    couch. About how much will the
    fabric for each cushion cost?

    ▮ about

    6) $17.53 ⟶)_____

22. A set of dishes costs $7.75. Teng
    ordered 8 sets. About how much
    did Teng spend on dishes?

    $7.75 ⟶
    × 8 ⟶
    _____
    ▮ about

23. One pair of socks cost $3.29.
    Dave bought 4 pairs of socks.
    About how much money in
    all did Dave spend?

    $3.29 ⟶
    × 4 ⟶
    _____
    ▮ about

24. Carlo spent $44.62 at the
    pizza shop. He bought 5 pizzas.
    About how much did each
    pizza cost?

    ▮ about

    5) $44.62 ⟶)_____

25. Larry spent $63.34 on movie tapes.
    He bought 7 tapes. About how much
    did each tape cost?

    ▮ about

    7) $63.34 ⟶)_____

5 Understanding Fractions

▼   ▼   ▼   ▼   ▼   ▼   ▼

At Kevin's party, the pan of brownies was cut into 8 equal pieces. Write a fraction to tell what part 1 brownie is to the whole pan.

Solve

▷ Write a problem about fractions and something to share.

_____

_____

_____

The Meaning of Fractions

A **fraction** names a part of a whole.
This whole is divided into 5 equal parts. 2 parts are brown.

$$\frac{1}{5}\ \frac{1}{5}\ \frac{1}{5}\ \frac{1}{5}\ \frac{1}{5}$$

$\dfrac{2}{5}$ ◄— brown parts
◄— total number of equal parts

A fraction also can name part of a group.
In this group of 4 circles, 1 circle is brown.

$\dfrac{1}{4}$ ◄— brown circle
◄— total circles in the group

A fraction has a **numerator** and a **denominator**. The numerator is the top number. The denominator is the bottom number.

$\dfrac{2}{3}$ ◄— numerator
◄— denominator

Guided Practice

▷ Write the fraction in the box that tells what part is brown.

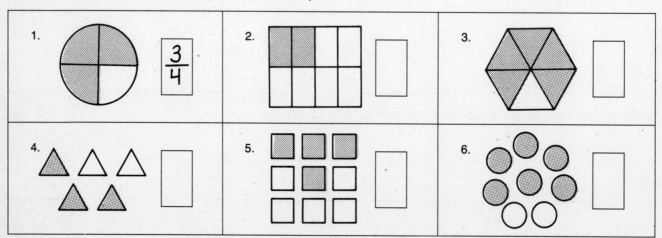

1. $\dfrac{3}{4}$

2.

3.

4.

5.

6.

94

Practice

▷ Write the fraction in the box that tells what part is brown.

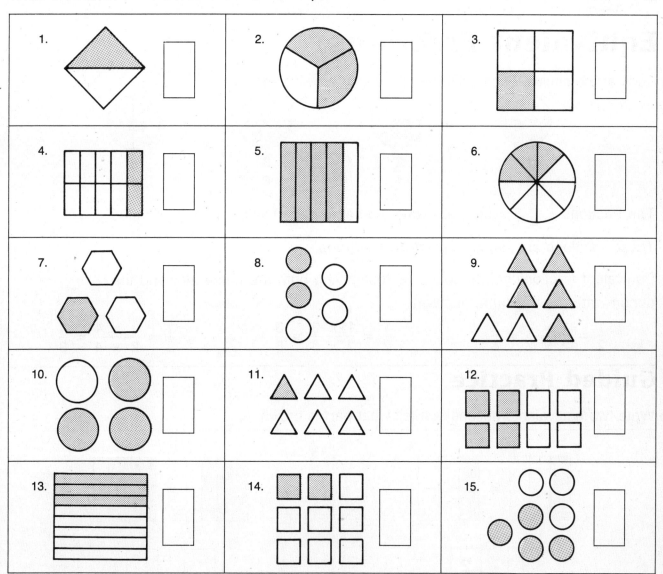

Using Math

▷ There are 12 books on the shelf. Peter has read 5 of the 12 books. Write a fraction that tells what part of the books Peter has read.

Peter has read _____ of the books.

Equivalent Fractions

Look at the circles. Each circle has the same brown part.

$\frac{1}{2}$

$\frac{2}{4}$

$\frac{3}{6}$

$\frac{4}{8}$

The fractions $\frac{1}{2}$, $\frac{2}{4}$, $\frac{3}{6}$, and $\frac{4}{8}$ all name the same part. They are equal in value.

These fractions are called **equivalent fractions**.

Equivalent fractions can be found by multiplying both the numerator and the denominator by the same number.

$$\frac{1}{2} = \frac{1 \times 2}{2 \times 2} = \frac{2}{4} \qquad \frac{1}{2} = \frac{1 \times 3}{2 \times 3} = \frac{3}{6} \qquad \frac{1}{2} = \frac{1 \times 4}{2 \times 4} = \frac{4}{8}$$

Guided Practice

▷ Write two equivalent fractions that tell what part is brown.

1.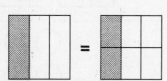

$$\frac{1}{3} = \frac{2}{6}$$

2.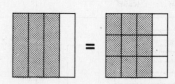

$$\boxed{} = \boxed{}$$

▷ Write three equivalent fractions for $\frac{1}{4}$.

3. $\frac{1}{4} = \frac{1 \times 2}{4 \times 2} = \boxed{\frac{2}{8}}$

4. $\frac{1}{4} = \frac{1 \times 3}{4 \times 3} = \boxed{}$

5. $\frac{1}{4} = \frac{1 \times 4}{4 \times 4} = \boxed{}$

Practice

▷ Write two equivalent fractions that tell what part is brown.

1.
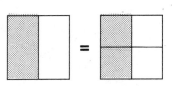

$$\Box = \Box$$

2.
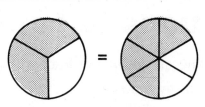

$$\Box = \Box$$

▷ Write an equivalent fraction.

3. $\dfrac{1}{3} = \dfrac{1 \times 2}{3 \times 2} = \Box$	4. $\dfrac{2}{5} = \dfrac{2 \times 2}{5 \times 2} = \Box$	5. $\dfrac{3}{4} = \dfrac{3 \times 2}{4 \times 2} = \Box$
6. $\dfrac{1}{3} = \dfrac{1 \times 3}{3 \times 3} = \Box$	7. $\dfrac{2}{5} = \dfrac{2 \times 3}{5 \times 3} = \Box$	8. $\dfrac{3}{4} = \dfrac{3 \times 3}{4 \times 3} = \Box$
9. $\dfrac{1}{3} = \dfrac{1 \times 4}{3 \times 4} = \Box$	10. $\dfrac{2}{5} = \dfrac{2 \times 4}{5 \times 4} = \Box$	11. $\dfrac{3}{4} = \dfrac{3 \times 4}{4 \times 4} = \Box$

Problem Solving

▷ Round to the nearest dollar.

Estimate to solve.

Plums cost $1.19 a pound. Yolanda bought
6 pounds of plums. About how much
money in all did Yolanda spend on plums?

$1.19 $\longrightarrow$

$\times\ 6$ $\longrightarrow$ $\times$ _____

 about

Fractions in Lowest Terms

You can find an equivalent fraction by dividing both the numerator and the denominator by the same number.

$$\frac{6}{9} = \frac{6 \div 3}{9 \div 3} = \frac{2}{3}$$

The fractions $\frac{6}{9}$ and $\frac{2}{3}$ are equivalent fractions. The fraction $\frac{2}{3}$ is in **lowest terms**. A fraction is in lowest terms when the numerator and denominator can only be divided by 1.

To reduce a fraction to lowest terms, divide the numerator and the denominator by the largest number that can divide both of them evenly (no remainders).

Reduce $\frac{8}{16}$ to lowest terms.

Think: What is the largest number that can divide both 8 and 16 evenly? Is it 2, 4, or 8? 8 is the largest number.

$$\frac{8}{16} = \frac{8 \div 8}{16 \div 8} = \frac{1}{2} \longleftarrow \text{lowest terms}$$

Guided Practice

▶ Write an equivalent fraction for each.

1.	2.	3.
$\frac{5}{10} = \frac{5 \div 5}{10 \div 5} = \boxed{\frac{1}{2}}$	$\frac{4}{8} = \frac{4 \div 2}{8 \div 2} = \boxed{}$	$\frac{2}{4} = \frac{2 \div 2}{4 \div 2} = \boxed{}$

▶ Complete to reduce each fraction to lowest terms.

4.	5.	6.
$\frac{6}{12} = \frac{6 \div \boxed{6}}{12 \div \boxed{6}} = \boxed{\frac{1}{2}}$	$\frac{9}{27} = \frac{9 \div \boxed{}}{27 \div \boxed{}} = \boxed{}$	$\frac{16}{24} = \frac{16 \div \boxed{}}{24 \div \boxed{}} = \boxed{}$

Practice

Write an equivalent fraction for each.

1. $\dfrac{3}{6} = \dfrac{3 \div 3}{6 \div 3} = \boxed{}$	2. $\dfrac{4}{12} = \dfrac{4 \div 4}{12 \div 4} = \boxed{}$	3. $\dfrac{8}{12} = \dfrac{8 \div 4}{12 \div 4} = \boxed{}$
4. $\dfrac{7}{14} = \dfrac{7 \div 7}{14 \div 7} = \boxed{}$	5. $\dfrac{5}{20} = \dfrac{5 \div 5}{20 \div 5} = \boxed{}$	6. $\dfrac{6}{8} = \dfrac{6 \div 2}{8 \div 2} = \boxed{}$

Complete to reduce each fraction to lowest terms.

7. $\dfrac{2}{4} = \dfrac{2 \div \boxed{}}{4 \div \boxed{}} = \boxed{}$	8. $\dfrac{4}{8} = \dfrac{4 \div \boxed{}}{8 \div \boxed{}} = \boxed{}$	9. $\dfrac{6}{10} = \dfrac{6 \div \boxed{}}{10 \div \boxed{}} = \boxed{}$
10. $\dfrac{5}{15} = \dfrac{5 \div \boxed{}}{15 \div \boxed{}} = \boxed{}$	11. $\dfrac{16}{20} = \dfrac{16 \div \boxed{}}{20 \div \boxed{}} = \boxed{}$	12. $\dfrac{25}{35} = \dfrac{25 \div \boxed{}}{35 \div \boxed{}} = \boxed{}$
13. $\dfrac{6}{9} = \dfrac{6 \div \boxed{}}{9 \div \boxed{}} = \boxed{}$	14. $\dfrac{9}{12} = \dfrac{9 \div \boxed{}}{12 \div \boxed{}} = \boxed{}$	15. $\dfrac{15}{25} = \dfrac{15 \div \boxed{}}{25 \div \boxed{}} = \boxed{}$

Using Math

It is 12 miles from Lori's house to Castle Hill Beach. Lori and her mother have already driven 4 miles. What fraction of the miles have they driven on their trip to the beach? Reduce the fraction to lowest terms.

Work here.

They have driven _____ of the miles.

Comparing Fractions

When two fractions have the same denominator, they are called **like fractions**. Only the numerators are used to compare like fractions.

Which fraction is greater: $\frac{2}{3}$ or $\frac{1}{3}$?

Since 2 is greater than 1, $\frac{2}{3} > \frac{1}{3}$.

$\frac{2}{3}$ [shaded rectangle diagram] $\frac{1}{3}$ [shaded rectangle diagram]

Fractions that have different denominators are called **unlike fractions**. To compare unlike fractions, first change them to like fractions. Then compare the numerators.

Which fraction is greater: $\frac{2}{3}$ or $\frac{1}{6}$?	Which fraction is less: $\frac{2}{3}$ or $\frac{3}{4}$?
Step 1 Find the equivalent fraction for $\frac{2}{3}$ that has a denominator of 6. $$\frac{2}{3} = \frac{?}{6}$$ Since $3 \times 2 = 6$, multiply the numerator and denominator by 2. $$\frac{2}{3} = \frac{2 \times 2}{3 \times 2} = \frac{4}{6}$$	**Step 1** Find equivalent fractions for both $\frac{2}{3}$ and $\frac{3}{4}$ that have the same denominator. 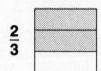 $$\frac{2}{3} \longrightarrow \frac{4}{6} = \frac{6}{9} = \left(\frac{8}{12}\right)$$ $$\frac{3}{4} \longrightarrow \frac{6}{8} = \left(\frac{9}{12}\right)$$
Step 2 Compare $\frac{4}{6}$ and $\frac{1}{6}$. $$\frac{4}{6} > \frac{1}{6}, \text{ so } \frac{2}{3} > \frac{1}{6}$$	**Step 2** Compare $\frac{8}{12}$ and $\frac{9}{12}$. $$\frac{8}{12} < \frac{9}{12}, \text{ so } \frac{2}{3} < \frac{3}{4}$$

Guided Practice

▶ Compare the fractions. Write >, <, or = in the box.

1. $\frac{1}{3} \boxed{<} \frac{4}{6}$ $\frac{1}{3} = \frac{2}{6}$	2. $\frac{1}{6} \square \frac{1}{8}$

Practice

▷ Compare the fractions. Write >, <, or = in the box.

1. $\dfrac{1}{2}$ ☐ $\dfrac{1}{4}$	2. $\dfrac{2}{5}$ ☐ $\dfrac{8}{10}$
3. $\dfrac{1}{3}$ ☐ $\dfrac{4}{9}$	4. $\dfrac{1}{16}$ ☐ $\dfrac{3}{8}$
5. $\dfrac{5}{6}$ ☐ $\dfrac{3}{4}$	6. $\dfrac{1}{2}$ ☐ $\dfrac{10}{20}$
7. $\dfrac{2}{6}$ ☐ $\dfrac{1}{3}$	8. $\dfrac{2}{15}$ ☐ $\dfrac{2}{3}$

Using Math

▷ Seth is making popovers for dinner. Will he use more or less salt than melted butter?

Work here.

Popover Recipe

2 eggs   ¼ teaspoon of salt
7/8 cup milk   ½ teaspoon of melted butter
1 cup flour

Seth will use _____ salt than melted butter.
                    more   less

Improper Fractions and Mixed Numbers

When the numerator of a fraction is equal to or greater than the denominator, the fraction is called an **improper fraction**.

You can write an improper fraction like $\frac{4}{4}$ as a whole number.

$$\frac{4}{4} = 1$$

You can write an improper fraction like $\frac{9}{4}$ as a whole number and a fraction.

This is called a **mixed number**.

To change an improper fraction to a mixed number, divide the numerator by the denominator. Then write the remainder over the denominator.

$$\frac{9}{4} \longrightarrow 4\overline{)9} \longrightarrow 2\frac{1}{4}$$
$$\underline{-8}$$
$$1 \longleftarrow \text{remainder}$$

Guided Practice

▶Change each improper fraction to a whole number or mixed number in lowest terms.

1. $\frac{4}{3} = \underline{1\frac{1}{3}}$ $\begin{array}{r} 1\frac{1}{3} \\ 3\overline{)4} \\ \underline{3} \\ 1 \end{array}$	2. $\frac{7}{2} = \underline{\hspace{1cm}}$	3. $\frac{5}{5} = \underline{\hspace{1cm}}$

Practice

▷ Change each improper fraction to a whole number or mixed number in lowest terms.

1. $\dfrac{2}{2}$ = _____	2. $\dfrac{7}{5}$ = _____	3. $\dfrac{5}{4}$ = _____
4. $\dfrac{15}{7}$ = _____	5. $\dfrac{15}{10}$ = _____	6. $\dfrac{12}{6}$ = _____
7. $\dfrac{10}{3}$ = _____	8. $\dfrac{36}{4}$ = _____	9. $\dfrac{17}{2}$ = _____
10. $\dfrac{14}{4}$ = _____	11. $\dfrac{9}{4}$ = _____	12. $\dfrac{21}{3}$ = _____

Using Math

▷ Seven friends each ate $\dfrac{1}{4}$ of an apple.

How many apples were eaten?

_____ apples were eaten.

Work here.

103

Fractions and Decimals

A fraction can be written as a decimal.

A fraction that has 10 or 100 as a denominator is easy to change to a decimal.

3 tenths

47 hundredths

$$\frac{3}{10} = 0.3$$

$$\frac{47}{100} = 0.47$$

To change other fractions to decimals, divide the numerator by the denominator.

$$\frac{3}{8} \longrightarrow 8\overline{)3.000}^{\;0.375} \longrightarrow 0.375$$

To change a mixed number to a decimal, find the decimal for the fraction. Then, add the decimal and the whole number.

$$1\frac{1}{2} \longrightarrow 2\overline{)1.0}^{\;0.5} \qquad \begin{array}{r} 0.5 \\ +1.0 \\ \hline 1.5 \end{array} \longrightarrow 1.5$$

Guided Practice

▶ Change each fraction or mixed number to a decimal.

1. $2\frac{3}{6} = \underline{\;2.5\;}$	2. $\frac{9}{100} = \underline{\qquad}$	3. $\frac{3}{5} = \underline{\qquad}$
$6\overline{)3.0}^{\;0.5}$ $\begin{array}{r}0.5\\+2.0\\\hline 2.5\end{array}$ $\begin{array}{r}-30\\\hline 0\end{array}$		

Practice

▷ Change each fraction or mixed number to a decimal.

1. $\frac{3}{10}$ = _____	2. $\frac{45}{100}$ = _____	3. $\frac{8}{100}$ = _____
4. $\frac{3}{4}$ = _____	5. $\frac{1}{4}$ = _____	6. $\frac{5}{8}$ = _____
7. $1\frac{8}{10}$ = _____	8. $2\frac{25}{100}$ = _____	9. $2\frac{1}{10}$ = _____
10. $1\frac{1}{5}$ = _____	11. $1\frac{3}{5}$ = _____	12. $4\frac{1}{2}$ = _____

Using Math

▷ Kimberlee went to the store to buy $\frac{3}{4}$ of a pound of sliced ham.

The ham was weighed on a scale showing decimal weights.

What number showed on the scale? _____

Work here.

Cups, Pints, Quarts, and Gallons

Cups, **pints**, **quarts**, and **gallons** are units used to measure liquid capacity, or how much a container holds.

| 2 cups = 1 pint |
| 4 cups = 1 quart |

2 pints = 1 quart

4 pints = $\frac{1}{2}$ gallon

8 pints = 1 gallon

2 quarts = $\frac{1}{2}$ gallon

4 quarts = 1 gallon

To change a larger unit to a smaller unit, such as gallons to quarts, multiply.

3 gallons = $\underline{\ ?\ }$ quarts

3 × 4 = 12 quarts

$\overline{\text{4 quarts = 1 gallon}}$

To change a smaller unit to a larger unit, such as cups to quarts, divide.

12 cups = $\underline{\ ?\ }$ quarts

12 ÷ 4 = 3 quarts

$\overline{\text{4 cups = 1 quart}}$

Guided Practice

▷ Complete.

1. 8 pints = _16_ cups

2. 6 pints = _____ quarts

3. 5 quarts = _____ pints

4. 8 cups = _____ quarts

5. 2 gallons = _____ quarts

6. 12 quarts = _____ gallons

106

Practice

▷ Complete.

1. 4 pints = _____ cups

2. 10 cups = _____ pints

3. 3 quarts = _____ cups

4. 2 pints = _____ quart

5. 7 quarts = _____ pints

6. 16 pints = _____ quarts

7. 1 gallon = _____ quarts

8. 8 quarts = _____ gallons

9. 9 gallons = _____ quarts

10. 16 cups = _____ quarts

11. 12 gallons = _____ pints

12. 4 quarts = _____ gallon

13. $\frac{1}{2}$ gallon = _____ quarts

14. 4 pints = _____ gallon

15. 8 cups = _____ pints

16. 16 quarts = _____ gallons

17. 12 quarts = _____ gallons

18. 8 pints = _____ quarts

19. 8 gallons = _____ quarts

20. 2 gallons = _____ pints

Using Math

▷ Ms. Page needs 2 gallons of paint to repaint the classroom walls. The store only has quart containers of the color she needs. How many quarts of paint should she buy?

Work here.

She should buy _____ quarts of paint.

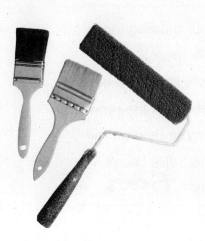

107

 **Problem Solving**

Identify Extra Information

Sometimes a problem gives you more information
than you need to solve it.

For lemon salad dressing, Ann needs $\frac{1}{4}$ cup of lemon juice
and $\frac{1}{4}$ cup of olive oil. She also needs $\frac{1}{2}$ teaspoon
of salt and $\frac{1}{8}$ teaspoon of pepper. **Does Ann need
more salt or pepper?**

Step 1 Find the **facts you need**.

Ann needs $\frac{1}{2}$ teaspoon of salt and $\frac{1}{8}$ teaspoon of pepper.

Step 2 Cross out the **facts you do not need**.

~~Ann needs $\frac{1}{4}$ cup of lemon juice and $\frac{1}{4}$ cup of olive oil.~~

Step 3 Solve the problem.

$\frac{1}{2}$ teaspoon of salt is more than $\frac{1}{8}$ teaspoon of pepper.

$$\frac{1}{2} > \frac{1}{8}$$

Ann needs more __salt__.

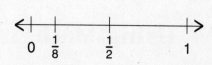

Guided Practice

▷ Cross out the fact you do not need.
Then solve the problem.

1. Kip spent $\frac{7}{8}$ hour mowing the
   Fiero's lawn. He spent $\frac{5}{8}$ hour
   mowing the Bell's lawn. ~~Kip used
   $\frac{1}{2}$ gallon of gasoline in the mower.~~
   Did Kip spend more time on the
   Fiero's or on the Bell's lawn?
   more time on the __Fiero's__ lawn

2. Ilsa ran $\frac{3}{4}$ mile on Saturday and
   $\frac{4}{4}$ mile on Sunday. She ran $\frac{3}{4}$ mile
   on Monday. Did Ilsa run farther
   on Saturday or Sunday?

   farther on _____

Practice

▷ Cross out the fact you do not need.
Then solve the problem.

---

1. Karena ate $\frac{3}{6}$ of a pizza, and Jesse ate $\frac{2}{6}$ of it. Mr. Perez ate $\frac{1}{6}$ of the pizza. Did Karena or Jesse eat more of the pizza?

   _____ ate more.

2. During the last hour of the school day, $\frac{3}{16}$ of Ms. Turner's class is in music, and $\frac{5}{16}$ of the class is in gym. $\frac{6}{16}$ of Ms. Turner's class stays after school for meetings. Is more of Ms. Turner's class in music or gym during the last hour?

   more in _____

3. Rob needs $\frac{3}{4}$ yard of yellow ribbon for a craft project. He has $\frac{7}{8}$ yard of blue ribbon and $\frac{6}{8}$ yard of green ribbon. Does Rob have more blue or green ribbon?

   more _____ ribbon

4. One moth is $\frac{8}{10}$ inch long. A ladybug is $\frac{2}{10}$ inch long. A large flea is $\frac{3}{10}$ inch long. Is the moth or the flea longer?

   _____ is longer

5. Elena walks $\frac{7}{10}$ mile to school. Phil walks $\frac{4}{10}$ mile to school. Jerome walks $\frac{5}{10}$ mile to school. Does Elena or Jerome walk farther to get to school?

   _____ walks farther.

6. Mr. Carswell mowed $\frac{6}{12}$ of his yard. Then Raymond mowed $\frac{5}{12}$ of the yard. Lee mowed $\frac{1}{12}$ of the yard. Did Mr. Carswell or Raymond mow more of the yard?

   _____ mowed more.

CHAPTER 5 Review

▷ Write the fraction that tells what part is brown. pages 94–95

1. 	2.	3.
4. 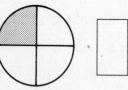	5.	6. 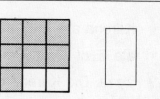

▷ Write an equivalent fraction. pages 96–97

7. $\dfrac{1}{2} = \dfrac{1 \times 2}{2 \times 2} = \boxed{}$	8. $\dfrac{2}{3} = \dfrac{2 \times 2}{3 \times 2} = \boxed{}$	9. $\dfrac{3}{4} = \dfrac{3 \times 3}{4 \times 3} = \boxed{}$
10. $\dfrac{4}{7} = \dfrac{4 \times 2}{7 \times 2} = \boxed{}$	11. $\dfrac{4}{7} = \dfrac{4 \times 3}{7 \times 3} = \boxed{}$	12. $\dfrac{4}{7} = \dfrac{4 \times 4}{7 \times 4} = \boxed{}$

▷ Complete to reduce each fraction to lowest terms. pages 98–99

13. $\dfrac{3}{6} = \dfrac{3 \div \boxed{}}{6 \div \boxed{}} = \boxed{}$	14. $\dfrac{4}{16} = \dfrac{4 \div \boxed{}}{16 \div \boxed{}} = \boxed{}$	15. $\dfrac{5}{10} = \dfrac{5 \div \boxed{}}{10 \div \boxed{}} = \boxed{}$
16. $\dfrac{6}{9} = \dfrac{6 \div \boxed{}}{9 \div \boxed{}} = \boxed{}$	17. $\dfrac{8}{24} = \dfrac{8 \div \boxed{}}{24 \div \boxed{}} = \boxed{}$	18. $\dfrac{25}{30} = \dfrac{25 \div \boxed{}}{30 \div \boxed{}} = \boxed{}$

▷ Compare the fractions. Write >, <, or = in the box.   pages 100–101

19. $\dfrac{3}{4}$ ☐ $\dfrac{2}{4}$	20. $\dfrac{7}{9}$ ☐ $\dfrac{8}{9}$	21. $\dfrac{4}{8}$ ☐ $\dfrac{1}{2}$
22. $\dfrac{1}{2}$ ☐ $\dfrac{4}{10}$	23. $\dfrac{4}{6}$ ☐ $\dfrac{2}{3}$	24. $\dfrac{5}{12}$ ☐ $\dfrac{7}{8}$

▷ Change each improper fraction to a whole number or mixed number in
lowest terms.   pages 102–103

25. $\dfrac{22}{5} =$ _____	26. $\dfrac{16}{2} =$ _____	27. $\dfrac{28}{8} =$ _____

▷ Change each fraction or mixed number to a decimal.   pages 104–105

28. $\dfrac{3}{8} =$ _____	29. $\dfrac{7}{10} =$ _____	30. $2\dfrac{9}{30} =$ _____

▷ Complete.   pages 106–107

31. 6 pints = _____ cups

32. 4 pints = _____ quarts

33. 8 quarts = _____ pints

34. 12 cups = _____ quarts

35. 5 gallons = _____ quarts

36. 2 quarts = _____ gallon

111

▶ Cross out the fact you do not need.
Then solve the problem. pages 108–109

37. Olga's class is planning a party. $\frac{2}{8}$ of the class wants cheese pizza. $\frac{1}{8}$ of the class wants pepperoni pizza. $\frac{5}{8}$ of the class wants vegetable pizza. Does more of the class want cheese pizza or vegetable pizza?

_____ pizza

38. Rick came home from school and spent $\frac{5}{15}$ of his free time doing homework. He played basketball for $\frac{4}{15}$ of his free time. He practiced the saxophone for $\frac{6}{15}$ of his time. Did Rick spend more time on basketball or homework?

more time on _____

39. Sally charted the weather for one month. She found $\frac{1}{6}$ of the days were rainy. $\frac{3}{6}$ of the days were sunny. $\frac{2}{6}$ of the days were cloudy. Were more days cloudy or rainy?

more were _____

40. Jess bought prizes to give out at a party. $\frac{4}{12}$ of the prizes were coupons. $\frac{2}{12}$ of the prizes were music cassettes. $\frac{6}{12}$ of the prizes were candy. Were more prizes music cassettes or candy?

more were _____

41. Sean spent $\frac{1}{3}$ of his day making a clay pot. He spent $\frac{2}{3}$ of his day running errands. He spent $\frac{2}{3}$ of his evening going to a movie. Did Sean spend more time making a clay pot or running errands?

more time _____

42. Belinda Cisneros made a video tape for her mom. Belinda sang on $\frac{2}{5}$ of the video tape. $\frac{2}{5}$ of the video is of Belinda tap dancing. $\frac{1}{5}$ of the video is of Belinda playing the piano. Is more of the video tap dancing or playing the piano?

more of the video _____

▷ Write an equivalent fraction.

1. $\dfrac{1}{3} = \dfrac{1 \times 2}{3 \times 2} = \boxed{}$	2. $\dfrac{3}{4} = \dfrac{3 \times 3}{4 \times 3} = \boxed{}$	3. $\dfrac{4}{5} = \dfrac{4 \times 2}{5 \times 2} = \boxed{}$

▷ Complete to reduce each fraction to lowest terms.

4. $\dfrac{2}{4} = \dfrac{2 \div \boxed{}}{4 \div \boxed{}} = \boxed{}$	5. $\dfrac{3}{9} = \dfrac{3 \div \boxed{}}{9 \div \boxed{}} = \boxed{}$	6. $\dfrac{8}{12} = \dfrac{8 \div \boxed{}}{12 \div \boxed{}} = \boxed{}$

▷ Compare the fractions. Write >, <, or = in the box.

7. $\dfrac{4}{5} \; \boxed{} \; \dfrac{7}{5}$	8. $\dfrac{1}{4} \; \boxed{} \; \dfrac{1}{6}$

▷ Change each improper fraction to a whole number or mixed number.

9. $\dfrac{5}{4} =$ _____	10. $\dfrac{9}{3} =$ _____	11. $\dfrac{17}{6} =$ _____

▷ Change each fraction or mixed number to a decimal.

12. $\dfrac{9}{10} =$ _____	13. $\dfrac{3}{5} =$ _____	14. $1\dfrac{1}{4} =$ _____

▷ Complete.

15. 5 quarts = _____ pints   16. 8 quarts = _____ gallons

▶ Cross out the fact you do not need.

Then solve the problem.

---

17. $\frac{1}{6}$ of the people at the movie theater saw a science fiction movie. $\frac{4}{6}$ of the people saw a cartoon. $\frac{3}{6}$ of the people bought popcorn. Did more people see a science fiction movie or a cartoon?

    more saw a _____

18. It is $\frac{3}{10}$ mile from Abe's house to the post office. Abe lives $\frac{2}{10}$ mile from the deli and $\frac{5}{10}$ mile from the dentist. Does Abe live closer to the deli or the dentist?

    closer to the _____

---

19. Sung Hye has $\frac{7}{8}$ yard of wool fabric. She has $\frac{6}{8}$ yard of cotton fabric. She has $\frac{4}{8}$ yard of silk fabric. Does Sung Hye have more cotton or more silk?

    more _____

20. Charlie walked $\frac{11}{12}$ mile on Monday. He walked $\frac{9}{12}$ mile on Wednesday. He walked $\frac{10}{12}$ mile on Friday. Did Charlie walk farther on Monday or on Friday?

    farther on _____

---

21. Cliff used $\frac{1}{4}$ yard of tan yarn for his art project. He used $\frac{1}{4}$ yard of white tape. He used $\frac{2}{4}$ yard of green yarn. Did Cliff use more tan yarn or more green yarn for his project?

    more _____ yarn

22. Mrs. Chaparro's children are Maria, Alonzo, and Marty. Maria is $\frac{3}{7}$ of her mother's height. Marty is $\frac{6}{7}$ of her mother's height. Alonzo is $\frac{4}{7}$ of his mother's height. Is Maria or Marty taller?

    _____ is taller.

114

CHAPTER 6

Adding and Subtracting Fractions

▼   ▼   ▼   ▼   ▼   ▼   ▼

Dan plays violin in the school orchestra. 5/8 of the string section are violin players. 2/8 are viola players. What part of the string section are violin and viola players?

Solve

▷ Write a problem about members of a group or a team.

Adding Like Fractions

Like fractions have the same denominator, which is called a **common denominator**. When you add like fractions, add the numerators only.

$$\frac{1}{4} + \frac{1}{4}$$

Step 1	Add the numerators.	
Step 2	Write the sum of the numerators over the common denominator.	
Step 3	Reduce the fraction to lowest terms.	

$$\frac{1}{4}$$
$$+\frac{1}{4}$$
$$\frac{2}{4} = \frac{1}{2}$$

Guided Practice

▷ Add. Reduce each answer to lowest terms.

1.

$$\frac{2}{6} \quad + \quad \frac{3}{6} \quad = \quad \boxed{\frac{5}{6}}$$

2.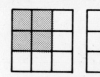

$$\frac{4}{9} \quad + \quad \frac{2}{9} \quad = \quad \boxed{} \quad = \quad \boxed{}$$

3.
$$\frac{5}{8}$$
$$+\frac{1}{8}$$
$$\boxed{} = \boxed{}$$

4.
$$\frac{2}{4}$$
$$+\frac{1}{4}$$
$$\boxed{}$$

5.
$$\frac{2}{10}$$
$$+\frac{6}{10}$$
$$\boxed{} = \boxed{}$$

6.
$$\frac{5}{7}$$
$$+\frac{2}{7}$$
$$\boxed{} = \boxed{}$$

116

Practice

▷ Add. Reduce each answer to lowest terms.

1. $\dfrac{1}{3}$ $+\dfrac{1}{3}$ ☐	2. $\dfrac{1}{8}$ $+\dfrac{3}{8}$ ☐ = ☐	3. $\dfrac{1}{4}$ $+\dfrac{1}{4}$ ☐ = ☐	4. $\dfrac{3}{9}$ $+\dfrac{1}{9}$ ☐	5. $\dfrac{4}{10}$ $+\dfrac{3}{10}$ ☐
6. $\dfrac{2}{7}$ $+\dfrac{3}{7}$ ☐	7. $\dfrac{2}{5}$ $+\dfrac{1}{5}$ ☐	8. $\dfrac{1}{6}$ $+\dfrac{1}{6}$ ☐ = ☐	9. $\dfrac{2}{10}$ $+\dfrac{3}{10}$ ☐ = ☐	10. $\dfrac{4}{9}$ $+\dfrac{4}{9}$ ☐
11. $\dfrac{1}{12}$ $+\dfrac{2}{12}$ ☐ = ☐	12. $\dfrac{4}{7}$ $+\dfrac{2}{7}$ ☐	13. $\dfrac{2}{9}$ $+\dfrac{1}{9}$ ☐ = ☐	14. $\dfrac{3}{10}$ $+\dfrac{6}{10}$ ☐	15. $\dfrac{3}{6}$ $+\dfrac{1}{6}$ ☐ = ☐

Using Math

▷ The school band is planning to raise money by washing cars. Kenny is
making 8 posters for the event. He finished making 4 of the posters on
Monday and 2 of the posters on Tuesday. What fraction of the 8 posters did
Kenny finish by Tuesday? Reduce your answer to lowest terms.

Kenny finished making _____ of the posters by Tuesday.

Subtracting Like Fractions

When you subtract like fractions, subtract the numerators only.

$$\frac{4}{6} - \frac{2}{6}$$

Step 1 Subtract the numerators.

Step 2 Write the difference of the numerators over the common denominator.

Step 3 Reduce the fraction to lowest terms.

$$\begin{array}{r} \frac{4}{6} \\ -\frac{2}{6} \\ \hline \frac{2}{6} = \frac{1}{3} \end{array}$$

Guided Practice

▷ Subtract. Reduce each answer to lowest terms.

1.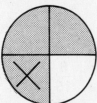

$$\frac{3}{4} - \frac{1}{4} = \boxed{\frac{2}{4}} = \boxed{\frac{1}{2}}$$

2.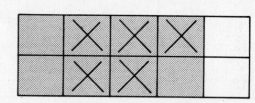

$$\frac{8}{10} - \frac{5}{10} = \boxed{}$$

3. $$\begin{array}{r} \frac{5}{6} \\ -\frac{2}{6} \\ \hline \end{array}$$ $\boxed{} = \boxed{}$

4. $$\begin{array}{r} \frac{6}{8} \\ -\frac{3}{8} \\ \hline \end{array}$$ $\boxed{}$

5. $$\begin{array}{r} \frac{8}{9} \\ -\frac{2}{9} \\ \hline \end{array}$$ $\boxed{} = \boxed{}$

6. $$\begin{array}{r} \frac{4}{5} \\ -\frac{3}{5} \\ \hline \end{array}$$ $\boxed{}$

Practice

▷ Subtract. Reduce each answer to lowest terms.

1. $\dfrac{3}{4}$ $-\dfrac{2}{4}$ ☐	2. $\dfrac{4}{6}$ $-\dfrac{2}{6}$ ☐ = ☐	3. $\dfrac{5}{8}$ $-\dfrac{2}{8}$ ☐	4. $\dfrac{4}{5}$ $-\dfrac{2}{5}$ ☐	5. $\dfrac{7}{8}$ $-\dfrac{3}{8}$ ☐ = ☐
6. $\dfrac{6}{8}$ $-\dfrac{4}{8}$ ☐ = ☐	7. $\dfrac{5}{9}$ $-\dfrac{2}{9}$ ☐ = ☐	8. $\dfrac{5}{6}$ $-\dfrac{4}{6}$ ☐	9. $\dfrac{7}{12}$ $-\dfrac{5}{12}$ ☐ = ☐	10. $\dfrac{8}{10}$ $-\dfrac{2}{10}$ ☐ = ☐
11. $\dfrac{6}{8}$ $-\dfrac{1}{8}$ ☐	12. $\dfrac{11}{12}$ $-\dfrac{2}{12}$ ☐ = ☐	13. $\dfrac{8}{9}$ $-\dfrac{2}{9}$ ☐ = ☐	14. $\dfrac{9}{10}$ $-\dfrac{4}{10}$ ☐ = ☐	15. $\dfrac{13}{16}$ $-\dfrac{9}{16}$ ☐ = ☐

Using Math

▷ Rita bought a dozen doughnuts. She gave 5 of the doughnuts to Pam and 3 of the doughnuts to Mary. How many more doughnuts did she give to Pam than to Mary?

Rita gave _____ more doughnuts to Pam than to Mary.
What fraction of the dozen doughnuts is that number?

The number is _____ of the dozen doughnuts.

119

Adding Unlike Fractions

Unlike fractions have different denominators. Before you add unlike fractions, find a common denominator. Then write an equivalent fraction using the common denominator. Add the like fractions.

$$\frac{2}{3} = \frac{4}{6}$$
$$+ \frac{1}{6} = \frac{1}{6}$$
$$\frac{5}{6}$$

Sometimes the sum of two fractions is an improper fraction. Change the improper fraction to a whole or a mixed number by dividing the numerator by the denominator. Reduce to lowest terms.

$$\frac{5}{12} = \frac{5}{12}$$
$$+ \frac{3}{4} = \frac{9}{12}$$
$$\frac{14}{12} = 1\frac{2}{12} = 1\frac{1}{6}$$

Guided Practice

▷ Add. Reduce the sum to lowest terms.

1.
$$\frac{1}{3} = \boxed{\frac{2}{6}}$$
$$+ \frac{2}{6} = \boxed{\frac{2}{6}}$$
$$\boxed{\frac{4}{6}} = \boxed{\frac{2}{3}}$$

2.
$$\frac{1}{2} = \boxed{}$$
$$+ \frac{4}{8} = \boxed{}$$
$$= \boxed{}$$

3.
$$\frac{6}{9} = \boxed{}$$
$$+ \frac{2}{3} = \boxed{}$$
$$= \boxed{} = \boxed{}$$

120

Practice

▷ Add. Reduce the sum to lowest terms.

1. $\dfrac{1}{5} = \boxed{}$ $+\dfrac{2}{10} = \boxed{}$ $\boxed{} = \boxed{}$	**2.** $\dfrac{3}{8} = \boxed{}$ $+\dfrac{1}{4} = \boxed{}$ $\boxed{}$	**3.** $\dfrac{1}{6} = \boxed{}$ $+\dfrac{1}{2} = \boxed{}$ $\boxed{} = \boxed{}$	**4.** $\dfrac{1}{2} = \boxed{}$ $+\dfrac{3}{8} = \boxed{}$ $\boxed{}$
5. $\dfrac{1}{6} = \boxed{}$ $+\dfrac{2}{3} = \boxed{}$ $\boxed{}$	**6.** $\dfrac{1}{5} = \boxed{}$ $+\dfrac{7}{15} = \boxed{}$ $\boxed{} = \boxed{}$	**7.** $\dfrac{3}{10} = \boxed{}$ $+\dfrac{2}{5} = \boxed{}$ $\boxed{}$	**8.** $\dfrac{8}{9} = \boxed{}$ $+\dfrac{1}{3} = \boxed{}$ $\boxed{} = \boxed{}$

9. $\dfrac{5}{6} = \boxed{}$ $+\dfrac{2}{3} = \boxed{}$ $\boxed{} = \boxed{} = \boxed{}$	**10.** $\dfrac{1}{2} = \boxed{}$ $+\dfrac{7}{8} = \boxed{}$ $\boxed{} = \boxed{}$	**11.** $\dfrac{1}{4} = \boxed{}$ $+\dfrac{11}{12} = \boxed{}$ $\boxed{} = \boxed{} = \boxed{}$

Subtracting Unlike Fractions

Before you can subtract unlike fractions, a common denominator must be found. Then write an equivalent fraction using the common denominator.

Subtract $\frac{3}{10}$ from $\frac{1}{2}$.

Step 1	Step 2	Step 3	Step 4
Find a common denominator.	Write an equivalent fraction for $\frac{1}{2}$.	Subtract the like fractions.	Reduce to lowest terms.
$\begin{array}{r} \frac{1}{2} \\ -\frac{3}{10} \\ \hline \end{array}$	$\begin{array}{r} \frac{1}{2} = \frac{5}{10} \\ -\frac{3}{10} = \frac{3}{10} \\ \hline \end{array}$	$\begin{array}{r} \frac{5}{10} \\ -\frac{3}{10} \\ \hline \frac{2}{10} \end{array}$	$\begin{array}{r} \frac{5}{10} \\ -\frac{3}{10} \\ \hline \frac{2}{10} = \frac{1}{5} \end{array}$

Guided Practice

▷ Subtract. Reduce the difference to lowest terms.

1.	2.	3.	4.
$\begin{array}{r} \frac{5}{8} = \boxed{\frac{5}{8}} \\ -\frac{1}{2} = \boxed{\frac{4}{8}} \\ \hline \boxed{\frac{1}{8}} \end{array}$	$\begin{array}{r} \frac{2}{3} = \boxed{} \\ -\frac{1}{6} = \boxed{} \\ \hline \boxed{} = \boxed{} \end{array}$	$\begin{array}{r} \frac{1}{6} = \boxed{} \\ -\frac{1}{12} = \boxed{} \\ \hline \boxed{} \end{array}$	$\begin{array}{r} \frac{2}{3} = \boxed{} \\ -\frac{3}{9} = \boxed{} \\ \hline \boxed{} = \boxed{} \end{array}$

Practice

▷ Subtract. Reduce the difference to lowest terms.

1. $\dfrac{7}{8}$ = ☐ $-\dfrac{3}{4}$ = ☐ —— ☐	**2.** $\dfrac{3}{10}$ = ☐ $-\dfrac{1}{5}$ = ☐ —— ☐	**3.** $\dfrac{5}{6}$ = ☐ $-\dfrac{1}{3}$ = ☐ —— ☐ = ☐	**4.** $\dfrac{5}{9}$ = ☐ $-\dfrac{1}{3}$ = ☐ —— ☐ = ☐
5. $\dfrac{7}{8}$ = ☐ $-\dfrac{5}{16}$ = ☐ —— ☐	**6.** $\dfrac{1}{2}$ = ☐ $-\dfrac{3}{10}$ = ☐ —— ☐ = ☐	**7.** $\dfrac{7}{9}$ = ☐ $-\dfrac{1}{3}$ = ☐ —— ☐	**8.** $\dfrac{1}{2}$ = ☐ $-\dfrac{5}{12}$ = ☐ —— ☐
9. $\dfrac{3}{5}$ = ☐ $-\dfrac{4}{15}$ = ☐ —— ☐ = ☐	**10.** $\dfrac{2}{3}$ = ☐ $-\dfrac{1}{12}$ = ☐ —— ☐	**11.** $\dfrac{7}{9}$ = ☐ $-\dfrac{5}{18}$ = ☐ —— ☐ = ☐	**12.** $\dfrac{4}{7}$ = ☐ $-\dfrac{2}{14}$ = ☐ —— ☐ = ☐

Adding Mixed Numbers

When you add mixed numbers, first add the fractions. Then add the whole numbers.

Add $2\frac{2}{9}$ and $1\frac{4}{9}$.

Step 1	Step 2	Step 3
Add the fractions.	Add the whole numbers.	Reduce to lowest terms.
$\begin{array}{r} 2\frac{2}{9} \\ +\ 1\frac{4}{9} \\ \hline \frac{6}{9} \end{array}$	$\begin{array}{r} 2\frac{2}{9} \\ +\ 1\frac{4}{9} \\ \hline 3\frac{6}{9} \end{array}$	$\begin{array}{r} 2\frac{2}{9} \\ +\ 1\frac{4}{9} \\ \hline 3\frac{6}{9} = 3\frac{2}{3} \end{array}$

Guided Practice

▷ Add. Reduce the sum to lowest terms.

1. $1\frac{3}{4} = \boxed{1\frac{3}{4}}$

   $+\ 3\frac{1}{2} = \boxed{3\frac{2}{4}}$

   $\boxed{4\frac{5}{4}} = \boxed{5\frac{1}{4}}$

2. $7\frac{1}{6} = \boxed{}$

   $+\ \frac{2}{3} = \boxed{}$

   $\boxed{}$

3. $2\frac{1}{8}$

   $+\ 6\frac{5}{8}$

   $\boxed{} = \boxed{}$

Practice

▷ Add. Reduce the sum to lowest terms.

1. $1\frac{3}{5}$ $+\ 1\frac{1}{5}$ ☐	**2.** $3\frac{1}{4}$ $+\ 2\frac{1}{4}$ ☐ = ☐	**3.** $6\frac{1}{6}$ $+\ \ \frac{3}{6}$ ☐ = ☐
4. $2\frac{1}{3}$ = ☐ $+\ 5\frac{1}{6}$ = ☐ ☐ = ☐	**5.** $3\frac{2}{9}$ = ☐ $+\ 3\frac{1}{3}$ = ☐ ☐	**6.** $4\frac{1}{4}$ = ☐ $+\ 3\frac{4}{8}$ = ☐ ☐ = ☐
7. $8\frac{1}{5}$ = ☐ $+\ 1\frac{2}{10}$ = ☐ ☐ = ☐	**8.** $2\frac{1}{12}$ = ☐ $+\ 1\frac{5}{6}$ = ☐ ☐	**9.** $3\frac{1}{3}$ = ☐ $+\ \ \frac{3}{6}$ = ☐ ☐

125

Subtracting Mixed Numbers

When you subtract mixed numbers, first subtract the fractions. Then subtract the whole numbers.

Subtract $1\frac{5}{12}$ from $5\frac{2}{3}$.

Step 1	Step 2	Step 3	Step 4
Find a common denominator and write the equivalent fraction.	Subtract the fractions.	Subtract the whole numbers.	Reduce the difference to lowest terms.
$5\frac{2}{3} = 5\frac{8}{12}$ $-\ 1\frac{5}{12} = 1\frac{5}{12}$	$5\frac{8}{12}$ $-\ 1\frac{5}{12}$ $\overline{\frac{3}{12}}$	$5\frac{8}{12}$ $-\ 1\frac{5}{12}$ $\overline{4\frac{3}{12}}$	$5\frac{8}{12}$ $-\ 1\frac{5}{12}$ $\overline{4\frac{3}{12} = 4\frac{1}{4}}$

Guided Practice

▶ Subtract. Reduce the difference to lowest terms.

1.
$$5\frac{7}{8} = \boxed{5\frac{7}{8}}$$
$$-\ 2\frac{1}{4} = \boxed{2\frac{2}{8}}$$
$$\boxed{3\frac{5}{8}}$$

2.
$$3\frac{4}{7}$$
$$-\ 1\frac{2}{7}$$
$$\boxed{}$$

3.
$$7\frac{1}{2} = \boxed{}$$
$$-\ \frac{3}{10} = \boxed{}$$
$$\boxed{} = \boxed{}$$

Practice

▷ Subtract. Reduce the difference to lowest terms.

1. $4\frac{3}{4}$ $-\ 1\frac{2}{4}$ ‒‒‒‒‒ $\boxed{}$	**2.** $6\frac{7}{9}$ $-\ 2\frac{2}{9}$ ‒‒‒‒‒ $\boxed{}$	**3.** $5\frac{1}{2} = \boxed{}$ $-\ 4\frac{1}{6} = \boxed{}$ ‒‒‒‒‒ $\boxed{}\ = \boxed{}$
4. $3\frac{7}{10} = \boxed{}$ $-\ 2\frac{1}{2} = \boxed{}$ ‒‒‒‒‒ $\boxed{}\ = \boxed{}$	**5.** $8\frac{3}{4} = \boxed{}$ $-\ 6\frac{3}{8} = \boxed{}$ ‒‒‒‒‒ $\boxed{}$	**6.** $6\frac{6}{8} = \boxed{}$ $-\ 1\frac{1}{4} = \boxed{}$ ‒‒‒‒‒ $\boxed{}\ = \boxed{}$
7. $10\frac{1}{2} = \boxed{}$ $-\ 5\frac{6}{14} = \boxed{}$ ‒‒‒‒‒ $\boxed{}$	**8.** $12\frac{7}{9} = \boxed{}$ $-\ 2\frac{1}{3} = \boxed{}$ ‒‒‒‒‒ $\boxed{}$	**9.** $15\frac{12}{16} = \boxed{}$ $-\ 12\frac{1}{4} = \boxed{}$ ‒‒‒‒‒ $\boxed{}\ = \boxed{}$

Ounces, Pounds, and Tons

Ounces, **pounds**, and **tons** are units used to measure weight.

A slice of bread weighs
about 1 ounce.

A loaf of bread weighs
about 1 pound.

Very heavy objects are measured in units called **tons**.

A compact car weighs about 1 ton.

16 ounces	=	1 pound
2,000 pounds	=	1 ton

To change a larger unit to a smaller unit, such as tons to pounds, multiply.	To change a smaller unit to a larger unit, such as ounces to pounds, divide.
2 tons = _?_ pounds 2 × 2,000 = 4,000 pounds ⌐2,000 pounds = 1 ton⌐	32 ounces = _?_ pounds 32 ÷ 16 = 2 pounds ⌐16 ounces = 1 pound⌐

Guided Practice

▷Ring the word that completes the sentence.

1. The Statue of Liberty weighs about 200 _____ .   ounces   pounds   tons

2. A pony weighs 500 _____ .   ounces   pounds   tons

▷Complete.

3. 2 pounds = _____ ounces   4. 5 tons = _____ pounds

128

Practice

▷ Ring the word to complete the sentence.

1. A tractor weighs about 8 ___.   ounce   pound   tons

2. A bag of flour weighs 5 ___.   ounces   pounds   tons

3. Your *Mastering Math* book weighs about 10 ___.   ounces   pounds   tons

4. A newborn baby weighs about 8 ___.   ounces   pounds   tons

5. An elephant weighs about 6 ___.   ounces   pounds   tons

▷ Complete.

6. 1 pound = _____ ounces

7. 3 pounds = _____ ounces

8. 160 ounces = _____ pounds

9. 2,000 pounds = _____ ton

10. 10 pounds = _____ ounces

11. 14 pounds = _____ ounces

12. 3 tons = _____ pounds

13. 320 ounces = _____ pounds

14. 15 pounds = _____ ounces

15. 8 tons = _____ pounds

Problem Solving

▷ Cross out the facts you do not need.
Then solve the problem.

Joel ran $\frac{3}{10}$ mile. Kyle ran $\frac{5}{10}$ mile. One lap around is $\frac{1}{4}$ mile. Did Joel or Kyle run farther? _____ ran farther.	Lauren used $\frac{4}{8}$ cup of oil to make salad dressing. She drank $\frac{1}{2}$ cup of water. She used $\frac{3}{8}$ cup of vinegar in the dressing. Did Lauren use more oil or more vinegar? more _____

 **Problem Solving**

Identify Extra Information

Sometimes a problem gives you more information
than you need to solve it.

Kelvin used $\frac{1}{2}$ cup of butter to make a cake.

He also used $\frac{1}{3}$ cup of oil, some sugar, and some flour.

Then Kelvin used $\frac{1}{2}$ cup of butter to make the frosting.

How much butter in all did Kelvin use?

> **Step 1** Find the **facts you need.**
> Kelvin used $\frac{1}{2}$ cup of butter in the cake and
> $\frac{1}{2}$ cup of butter in the frosting.

> **Step 2** Cross out the **facts you do not need.**
> ~~He also used $\frac{1}{3}$ cup of oil, some sugar, and some flour.~~

> **Step 3** Solve the problem.
> $\frac{1}{2}$ cup of butter in the cake
> $+\frac{1}{2}$ cup of butter in the frosting
> $\boxed{\frac{2}{2}} = \boxed{1}$ cup of butter in all

Guided Practice

▷ Cross out the fact you do not need.
Then solve the problem.

Bill ran $\frac{3}{10}$ mile. He walked $\frac{1}{2}$ mile.

Then he jogged $\frac{2}{10}$ mile. How much

farther did Bill run than he jogged?

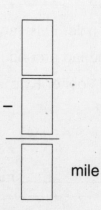 mile

Practice

▷ Cross out the fact you do not need.

Then solve the problem.

1. Derek bought $\frac{1}{4}$ pound of ham, $\frac{1}{4}$ pound of turkey, and $\frac{3}{4}$ pound of potato salad at the deli. How much meat in all did Derek buy?

$$+ \underline{}$$

pound

2. At Mo's Bakery, $\frac{3}{8}$ of the pies sold are apple, $\frac{3}{8}$ of the pies are pecan, and $\frac{1}{8}$ of the pies are blueberry. What fraction of the pies sold are apple and blueberry?

$$+ \underline{}$$

of the pies

3. Katya marked off a walking track in tenths of a mile. She put a yellow marker at $\frac{3}{10}$ mile and a blue marker at $\frac{6}{10}$ mile. She put a red marker at $\frac{9}{10}$ mile. What is the distance between the yellow and the blue markers?

$$- \underline{}$$

mile

4. Gina put different colors of sand in a 1-cup jar for an art project. First she used $\frac{1}{6}$ cup of tan sand. Then she used $\frac{1}{3}$ cup of blue sand and $\frac{1}{3}$ cup of pink sand. Then she used $\frac{1}{6}$ cup more of tan sand. How much tan sand in all did Gina use?

$$+ \underline{}$$

cup

5. Armando made cookies for his party. $\frac{1}{4}$ of the cookies were plain and $\frac{2}{4}$ of them were iced. $\frac{1}{4}$ of the cookies he made were chocolate chip. What fraction of the cookies Armando made were plain and iced?

$$+ \underline{}$$

cookies

6. Rachel bought $\frac{1}{2}$ pound of macaroni salad at the store. Then she bought $\frac{1}{3}$ pound of potato salad and $\frac{1}{3}$ pound of pea salad. How much potato salad and pea salad in all did Rachel buy?

$$+ \underline{}$$

pound

▷ Add. Reduce your answer to lowest terms.   pages 116–117

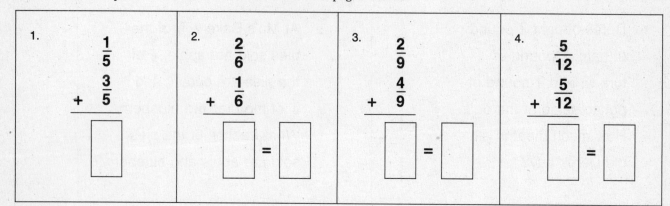

1.
$$\begin{array}{r} \frac{1}{5} \\ + \frac{3}{5} \\ \hline \ \ \end{array}$$

2.
$$\begin{array}{r} \frac{2}{6} \\ + \frac{1}{6} \\ \hline \ \ \end{array} = \ $$

3.
$$\begin{array}{r} \frac{2}{9} \\ + \frac{4}{9} \\ \hline \ \ \end{array} = \ $$

4.
$$\begin{array}{r} \frac{5}{12} \\ + \frac{5}{12} \\ \hline \ \ \end{array} = \ $$

▷ Subtract. Reduce your answer to lowest terms.   pages 118–119

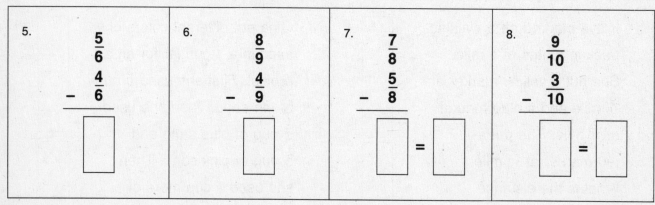

5.
$$\begin{array}{r} \frac{5}{6} \\ - \frac{4}{6} \\ \hline \ \ \end{array}$$

6.
$$\begin{array}{r} \frac{8}{9} \\ - \frac{4}{9} \\ \hline \ \ \end{array}$$

7.
$$\begin{array}{r} \frac{7}{8} \\ - \frac{5}{8} \\ \hline \ \ \end{array} = \ $$

8.
$$\begin{array}{r} \frac{9}{10} \\ - \frac{3}{10} \\ \hline \ \ \end{array} = \ $$

▷ Add. Reduce the sum to lowest terms.   pages 120–121

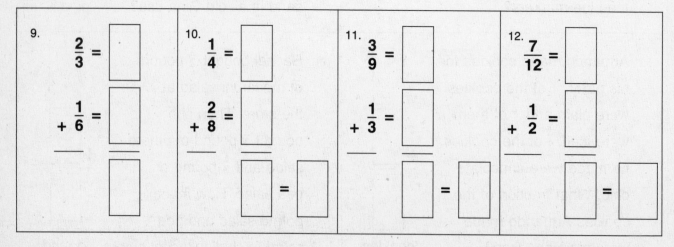

9.
$$\frac{2}{3} = \ $$
$$+ \frac{1}{6} = \ $$

10.
$$\frac{1}{4} = \ $$
$$+ \frac{2}{8} = \ $$
$$\ = \ $$

11.
$$\frac{3}{9} = \ $$
$$+ \frac{1}{3} = \ $$
$$\ = \ $$

12.
$$\frac{7}{12} = \ $$
$$+ \frac{1}{2} = \ $$
$$\ = \ $$

132

CHAPTER 6 Review

▷ Subtract. Reduce the difference to lowest terms. pages 122–123

13.
$$\frac{3}{4} = \boxed{}$$
$$-\frac{1}{2} = \boxed{}$$
$$\boxed{}$$

14.
$$\frac{5}{6} = \boxed{}$$
$$-\frac{1}{3} = \boxed{}$$
$$\boxed{} = \boxed{}$$

15.
$$\frac{1}{5} = \boxed{}$$
$$-\frac{1}{10} = \boxed{}$$
$$\boxed{}$$

16.
$$\frac{11}{12} = \boxed{}$$
$$-\frac{1}{6} = \boxed{}$$
$$\boxed{} = \boxed{}$$

▷ Add. Reduce the sum to lowest terms. pages 124–125

17.
$$2\frac{1}{3}$$
$$+ 2\frac{1}{3}$$
$$\boxed{}$$

18.
$$1\frac{1}{4} = \boxed{}$$
$$+ 4\frac{4}{8} = \boxed{}$$
$$\boxed{} = \boxed{}$$

19.
$$3\frac{5}{9} = \boxed{}$$
$$+ \frac{1}{3} = \boxed{}$$
$$\boxed{}$$

▷ Subtract. Reduce the difference to lowest terms. pages 126–127

20.
$$4\frac{4}{5}$$
$$- 1\frac{2}{5}$$
$$\boxed{}$$

21.
$$5\frac{6}{8} = \boxed{}$$
$$- \frac{1}{2} = \boxed{}$$
$$\boxed{} = \boxed{}$$

22.
$$8\frac{6}{7} = \boxed{}$$
$$- 2\frac{5}{14} = \boxed{}$$
$$\boxed{} = \boxed{}$$

▷ Complete. pages 128–129

23. 80 ounces = _____ pounds   24. 7 tons = _____ pounds   **133**

▶ Cross out the fact you do not need.

Then solve the problem. pages 130–131

---

25. Cleo used $\frac{6}{12}$ cup of white corn meal and $\frac{1}{12}$ cup of yellow corn meal to make corn bread. She also used $\frac{1}{3}$ cup of flour. How much corn meal in all did Cleo use?

$$\square + \square = \square$$

cup

---

26. Jenny used $\frac{3}{6}$ of a loaf of bread for sandwiches. She used $\frac{1}{6}$ of the loaf for toast. She used $\frac{2}{6}$ of the loaf for feeding ducks. How much of the loaf did Jenny use for toast and sandwiches?

$$\square + \square = \square$$

of the loaf

---

27. Joe lives $\frac{1}{5}$ mile from school. He lives $\frac{1}{2}$ mile from the park. It is $\frac{1}{2}$ mile from the park to the store. How far will Joe walk if he starts at home, goes to the park, and then to the store?

$$\square + \square = \square$$

mile

---

28. Ti walked $\frac{2}{8}$ mile to warm up. Then he ran 4 miles. Next Ti walked $\frac{3}{8}$ mile to cool down. How far in all did Ti walk?

$$\square + \square = \square$$

mile

---

29. Kevin used $\frac{1}{2}$ teaspoon of salt to make cookies. He used $\frac{2}{4}$ cup of flour and $\frac{1}{4}$ cup of sugar. How much more flour than sugar did Kevin use?

$$\square - \square = \square$$

cup

---

30. Cedar City School District has many buses. $\frac{2}{10}$ of the buses are in the shop for engine repairs. $\frac{2}{10}$ of the buses are in the shop for painting. $\frac{6}{10}$ of the buses are not in the shop. What fraction of the buses are in the shop?

$$\square + \square = \square$$

of the buses

Add or subtract. Reduce your answer to lowest terms.

1.
$$\begin{array}{r} \frac{3}{8} \\ + \frac{1}{8} \\ \hline \end{array}$$
☐ = ☐

2.
$$\begin{array}{r} \frac{5}{10} \\ + \frac{3}{10} \\ \hline \end{array}$$
☐ = ☐

3.
$$\begin{array}{r} \frac{7}{9} \\ - \frac{2}{9} \\ \hline \end{array}$$
☐

4.
$$\begin{array}{r} \frac{7}{6} \\ - \frac{5}{6} \\ \hline \end{array}$$
☐ = ☐

Add or subtract. Reduce the sum or difference to lowest terms.

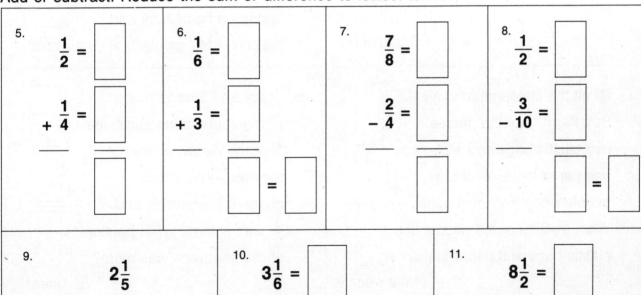

5.
$$\frac{1}{2} = ☐$$
$$+ \frac{1}{4} = ☐$$
$$☐$$

6.
$$\frac{1}{6} = ☐$$
$$+ \frac{1}{3} = ☐$$
$$☐ = ☐$$

7.
$$\frac{7}{8} = ☐$$
$$- \frac{2}{4} = ☐$$
$$☐$$

8.
$$\frac{1}{2} = ☐$$
$$- \frac{3}{10} = ☐$$
$$☐ = ☐$$

9.
$$2\frac{1}{5}$$
$$+ 1\frac{3}{5}$$
$$☐$$

10.
$$3\frac{1}{6} = ☐$$
$$+ 4\frac{1}{3} = ☐$$
$$☐ = ☐$$

11.
$$8\frac{1}{2} = ☐$$
$$- 4\frac{1}{8} = ☐$$
$$☐$$

Complete.

12. 16 ounces = _____ pound

13. 10 tons = _____ pounds

14. 16 pounds = _____ ounces

15. 6 tons = _____ pounds **135**

▷ Cross out the fact you do not need.

Then solve the problem.

16. Joli used $\frac{1}{8}$ teaspoon of pepper and $\frac{3}{8}$ teaspoon of salt. She added $\frac{3}{4}$ teaspoon of oregano. How much more salt did Joli use than pepper?

$-$

teaspoon

17. David spent $\frac{4}{5}$ of an hour on homework. He did chores for $\frac{1}{2}$ an hour. He also played video games for $\frac{2}{5}$ of an hour. How much time did David spend on homework and playing video games?

$+$

hour

18. Of all the shoppers at Buy Right, $\frac{1}{8}$ of the people use plastic bags and $\frac{4}{8}$ of them use paper bags. $\frac{2}{8}$ of the people bring their own bags. What fraction of the people use plastic bags and paper bags?

$+$

of the people

19. Tracy and Tyrone made a huge submarine sandwich. $\frac{1}{6}$ of the sandwich was tomatoes and $\frac{2}{6}$ was cheese. $\frac{2}{6}$ was ham and $\frac{1}{6}$ was salami. What fraction of the sandwich was meat?

$+$

meat

20. Molly buys $\frac{3}{4}$ pound of cheese. She buys $\frac{3}{4}$ pound of bacon and $\frac{1}{4}$ pound of sausage. How much bacon and sausage in all did Molly buy?

$+$

pound

21. Sabrina ran $\frac{1}{3}$ mile on Monday and $\frac{1}{3}$ mile on Tuesday. She also walked 3 miles both days. How far did Sabrina run Monday and Tuesday?

$+$

mile

7 Percents

A serving of one cup of skim milk provides 25% of your daily requirement of Vitamin D. What fractional part of your daily requirement is this?

Solve

▷ Write a problem about a good breakfast using percents.

Ratios

How many players out of 6 have caps?

5 out of 6 players have caps.

5 out of 6 is called a **ratio**. This ratio compares the
number of players with caps to the total number of players.

You can write a ratio as a fraction.

You read the ratio as *5 to 6*.

$\dfrac{5}{6}$ ⟵ players with caps
⟵ players in all

What is the ratio of girl players to boy players?

The ratio is 2 to 4.

$\dfrac{2}{4}$ ⟵ girl players
⟵ boy players

Since $\dfrac{2}{4} = \dfrac{1}{2}$, you also can say the ratio of girl players to boy players is 1 to 2.

Guided Practice

▷ Write each ratio as a fraction in lowest terms.

1. circles to all figures

2. triangles to squares ☐ or ☐

3. circles to triangles ☐

4. 7 days of rain to 30 days in a month ☐

5. 6 white poodles to 12 black poodles ☐ or ☐

Practice

▷ Write each ratio as a fraction in lowest terms.

1. brown stars to black stars

2. black stars to all stars [ ] or [ ]

3. white stars to black stars

4. brown stars to white stars [ ] or [ ]

5. white stars to all stars

6. 1 baseball bat to 9 players

7. 2 cups of rice to 6 cups of water [ ] or [ ]

8. 7 radios to 9 televisions

9. 15 students to 1 teacher

10. 9 desks to 12 chairs [ ] or [ ]

11. 17 science books to 20 math books

Using Math

▷ At the end of the month, the weatherman reported the weather for each day. He reported that 8 out of 31 days in May were sunny.

Write the ratio as a fraction. _____
What was the ratio of rainy days to sunny days? Write the ratio as a fraction.

_____ or _____

Weather in May	
	Number of days
Sunny	8
Cloudy	5
Partly Cloudy	12
Rainy	6

Percents

What is the ratio of brown parts to all 100 parts of the square?

The ratio is $\dfrac{25}{100}$ ← brown parts
← all parts of the square

When the denominator of a ratio is 100, you can write the ratio as a **percent**. Percent means *per hundred*. The symbol for percent is **%**.

$$\dfrac{25}{100} = 25 \text{ per hundred} = 25 \text{ percent or } \mathbf{25\%}$$

Guided Practice

▷ What the ratio of the brown parts to total parts.

1. $\dfrac{4}{100}$

2.

3.

▷ Write each ratio as a percent.

4. $\dfrac{5}{100} = \underline{\quad 5\% \quad}$

5. $\dfrac{18}{100} = \underline{\quad\quad}$

6. $\dfrac{75}{100} = \underline{\quad\quad}$

7. $\dfrac{20}{100} = \underline{\quad\quad}$

8. $\dfrac{66}{100} = \underline{\quad\quad}$

9. $\dfrac{44}{100} = \underline{\quad\quad}$

▷ Write each percent as a ratio.

10. $46\% = \dfrac{46}{100}$

11. $22\% =$

12. $100\% =$

13. $15\% =$

14. $88\% =$

15. $3\% =$

Practice

Write each ratio as a percent.

1. $\dfrac{12}{100}$ = _____

2. $\dfrac{7}{100}$ = _____

3. $\dfrac{25}{100}$ = _____

4. $\dfrac{10}{100}$ = _____

5. $\dfrac{82}{100}$ = _____

6. $\dfrac{1}{100}$ = _____

7. $\dfrac{50}{100}$ = _____

8. $\dfrac{4}{100}$ = _____

9. $\dfrac{100}{100}$ = _____

Write each percent as a ratio.

10. 5% =

11. 20% =

12. 35% =

13. 72% =

14. 2% =

15. 10% =

16. 1% =

17. 95% =

18. 40% =

Using Math

The school ordered 100 new books for the library. Mrs. Casper listed the number of new books by type of book. Write the ratio of mystery books to all new books. Then write the ratio as a percent.

Write your answer here.

_____ = _____

New Books

Type	Number of Books
Reference	22
Biographies	13
Other Nonfiction	12
Mystery	15
Other Fiction	38
Total	100

Ratios and Percents

When Paul unpacked a box of 25 glasses, 3 out of 25 were broken. The ratio of broken glasses to all glasses is 3 to 25, or $\frac{3}{25}$. What percent of the glasses were broken?

To write the ratio $\frac{3}{25}$ as a percent, find the equivalent ratio that has a denominator of 100.

What number times 25 is 100? $\quad \frac{3}{25} = \frac{?}{100}$

Step 1	Step 2	Step 3
Divide 100 by 25 to find the number you multiply by. $$25\overline{)100}^{\;4}$$	Multiply the numerator and the denominator by 4. $$\frac{3}{25} = \frac{3 \times 4}{25 \times 4} = \frac{12}{100}$$	Write the ratio as a percent. $$\frac{12}{100} = 12\%$$

12% of the glasses were broken.

Guided Practice

 Complete. Then write each ratio as a percent.

1. $\frac{2}{5} = \frac{2 \times 20}{5 \times 20} = \boxed{\frac{\boxed{40}}{100}} = \underline{40\%}$

2. $\frac{1}{50} = \frac{1 \times 2}{50 \times 2} = \frac{\boxed{}}{100} = \underline{}$

3. $\frac{3}{10} = \frac{3 \times \boxed{}}{10 \times \boxed{}} = \frac{\boxed{}}{100} = \underline{}$

4. $\frac{1}{2} = \frac{1 \times \boxed{}}{2 \times \boxed{}} = \frac{\boxed{}}{\boxed{}} = \underline{}$

Practice

▷ Complete. Then write each ratio as a percent.

1. $\dfrac{4}{10} = \dfrac{4 \times 10}{10 \times 10} = \dfrac{\boxed{}}{100} = $ _____	**2.** $\dfrac{3}{50} = \dfrac{3 \times 2}{50 \times 2} = \dfrac{\boxed{}}{100} = $ _____
3. $\dfrac{2}{25} = \dfrac{2 \times \boxed{}}{25 \times \boxed{}} = \dfrac{\boxed{}}{100} = $ _____	**4.** $\dfrac{3}{5} = \dfrac{3 \times \boxed{}}{5 \times \boxed{}} = \dfrac{\boxed{}}{100} = $ _____
5. $\dfrac{3}{4} = \dfrac{3 \times \boxed{}}{4 \times \boxed{}} = \dfrac{\boxed{}}{\boxed{}} = $ _____	**6.** $\dfrac{1}{2} = \dfrac{1 \times \boxed{}}{2 \times \boxed{}} = \dfrac{\boxed{}}{\boxed{}} = $ _____
7. $\dfrac{11}{20} = \dfrac{11 \times \boxed{}}{20 \times \boxed{}} = \dfrac{\boxed{}}{\boxed{}} = $ _____	**8.** $\dfrac{1}{5} = \dfrac{1 \times \boxed{}}{5 \times \boxed{}} = \dfrac{\boxed{}}{\boxed{}} = $ _____

Using Math

▷ Marvin took a magazine quiz called "Would You be a Good Pilot?" There were 10 questions. Marvin answered 8 correctly. Write his score as a percent.

Work here.

Marvin's score was _____.

Decimals and Percents

You can write a decimal as a percent or a percent as a decimal.

25 out of 100 parts are brown,
or $\frac{25}{100}$ are brown.

$$\frac{25}{100} = 25 \text{ hundredths} = 0.25 \text{ or } 25\%$$

These examples show how to write a decimal as a percent.

$$0.15 = 15 \text{ hundredths} = 15\%$$
$$0.09 = 9 \text{ hundredths} = 9\%$$

These examples show how to write a percent as a decimal.

$$56\% = 56 \text{ hundredths} = 0.56$$
$$8\% = 8 \text{ hundredths} = 0.08$$
$$20\% = 20 \text{ hundredths} = 0.20 \text{ or } 0.2$$

Guided Practice

▷ Complete.

1. 0.75 = ___75___ hundredths = ___75___ %

2. 0.03 = _____ hundredths = _____%

3. 10% = _____ hundredths = _____ or _____

4. 7% = _____ hundredths = _____

▷ Write each decimal as a percent.

5. 0.53 = __53%__   6. 0.09 = _____   7. 0.25 = _____

▷ Write each percent as a decimal.

8. 16% = __0.16__   9. 100% = _____ or _____   10. 1% = _____

Practice

▷ Write each decimal as a percent.

1. 0.23 = _____   2. 0.15 = _____   3. 0.39 = _____

4. 0.76 = _____   5. 0.02 = _____   6. 0.47 = _____

7. 0.05 = _____   8. 0.58 = _____   9. 0.08 = _____

10. 0.96 = _____   11. 0.33 = _____   12. 0.51 = _____

13. 0.88 = _____   14. 0.66 = _____   15. 0.20 = _____

▷ Write each percent as a decimal.

16. 14% = _____   17. 31% = _____   18. 5% = _____

19. 22% = _____   20. 6% = _____   21. 65% = _____

22. 9% = _____   23. 70% = _____ or _____   24. 99% = _____

25. 50% = _____ or _____   26. 48% = _____   27. 43% = _____

28. 7% = _____   29. 10% = _____   30. 80% = _____

Problem Solving

▷ Cross out the fact you do not need.
Then solve the problem.

Joana made a fruit shake with
$\frac{3}{4}$ cup of milk. She used $\frac{1}{2}$ cup of
strawberries and $\frac{1}{2}$ cup of peaches.
How many cups of fruit did Joana use?

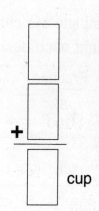

cup

Fractions, Decimals, and Percents

Fractions, decimals, and percents can name the same amounts.

$$\frac{37}{100} = 0.37 = 37\%$$

You can change the fraction $\frac{3}{4}$ to a percent by first changing the fraction to a decimal in hundredths.

Step 1		Step 2	
Divide the numerator by the denominator.	$\begin{array}{r} 0.75 \\ 4\overline{)3.00} \\ -2\,8 \\ \hline 20 \\ -20 \\ \hline 0 \end{array}$	Write the decimal as a percent.	$0.75 = 75\%$

Fraction	Decimal	Percent
$\frac{3}{4}$	0.75	75%

Guided Practice

▶ Complete the chart. You will need to do your work on your own paper.
Round each decimal to the nearest hundredth.

Fraction	Decimal	Percent
$\frac{32}{100}$	1. _0.32_	32%
$\frac{1}{4}$	0.25	2. _____
$\frac{1}{2}$	3. _____	4. _____
$\frac{4}{7}$	5. _____	6. _____

146

Practice

▷ Complete the chart. Round each decimal to the nearest hundredth.

Fraction	Decimal	Percent
$\frac{16}{100}$	0.16	1. _____
$\frac{9}{100}$	2. _____	9%
$\frac{27}{100}$	3. _____	4. _____
$\frac{1}{4}$	5. _____	6. _____
$\frac{1}{5}$	7. _____	8. _____
$\frac{5}{8}$	9. _____	10. _____
$\frac{4}{5}$	11. _____	12. _____
$\frac{3}{8}$	13. _____	14. _____
$\frac{2}{3}$	15. _____	16. _____
$\frac{3}{7}$	17. _____	18. _____

Using Math

▷ The students in Mr. Parker's class took a poll to see what kind of pets the class had. Complete the following sentences, writing **dogs**, **cats**, or **other** as your answer.

1. 25% of the students had _____ as pets.

2. 50% of the students had _____ as pets.

3. 20% of the students had _____ pets.

Our Pets	
Fraction of Class	Pet
$\frac{1}{2}$	Dogs
$\frac{1}{4}$	Cats
$\frac{1}{5}$	Other (Birds, Fish)

Percents of Numbers

The basketball team scored a total of 84 points. 25% of the points were foul shots. How many foul shots were scored?

Step 1 ▸ Write the percent as a decimal.	Step 2 ▸ Multiply.
25% = 0.25	8 4 ×0.2 5 —— 2 decimal places 4 2 0 1 6 8 0 2 1.0 0 —— 2 decimal places Drop zeros. 21.00 = 21

<u>25% of 84</u> points = 21 foul shots

Guided Practice

▸Find the percent of each number to complete the statement. You will need to do your work on your own paper.

1. <u>8% of 50</u> students were born in October. ___4___ students were born in October.

2. <u>35% of 20</u> roses are red. _____ roses are red.

3. <u>60% of 24</u> hours are spent awake. _____ hours are spent awake.

4. 100% of 49 = _____

5. 15% of 23 = _____

6. 80% of 20 = _____

7. 42% of 55 = _____

148

Practice

▷Find the percent of each number.

1. 10% of 30 = _____

2. 4% of 50 = _____

3. 75% of 28 = _____

4. 20% of 35 = _____

5. 32% of 75 = _____

6. 10% of 60 = _____

7. 15% of 70 = _____

8. 90% of 15 = _____

9. 45% of 92 = _____

10. 60% of 95 = _____

11. 25% of 100 = _____

12. 33% of 88 = _____

13. 30% of 150 = _____

14. 56% of 38 = _____

15. 48% of 52 = _____

16. 17% of 17 = _____

Using Math

▷David earns $65 each month mowing lawns. He is planning
how he will spend some of the money. He is also planning
how much money he will save. David has made a list
showing the percent he will put aside for each item. How
much money does David plan to put in savings each
month?

David plans to put _____ in savings each month.

Work here.

25% – Gasoline for mower
40% – Movies and other spending money
20% – Savings
15% – Airplane Model collection

149

Grams and Kilograms

Grams and **kilograms** are metric units used to measure the weight of an object.

Lighter objects are measured in grams.

A safety pin weighs about
1 gram.

Heavier objects are measured in kilograms.

A tennis racket weighs about
1 kilogram.

1,000 grams = 1 kilogram

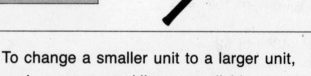

To change a larger unit to a smaller unit, such as kilograms to grams, multiply.	To change a smaller unit to a larger unit, such as grams to kilograms, divide.
2 kilograms = __?__ grams 2 × 1,000 = 2,000 grams 1,000 grams = 1 kilogram	2,000 grams = __?__ kilograms 2,000 ÷ 1,000 = 2 kilograms 1,000 grams = 1 kilogram

Guided Practice

▷ Ring the word that completes the sentence.

1. A bicycle weighs about 20 ___.   grams   kilograms

2. A penny weighs about 3 ___.   grams   kilograms

▷ Complete.

3. 3 kilograms = _____ grams

4. 8,000 grams = _____ kilograms

5. 15 kilograms = _____ grams

6. 10,000 grams = _____ kilograms

150

Practice

▷ Ring the word that completes the sentence.

1. A pencil weighs about 4 ___.   grams   kilograms

2. A sheet of paper weighs about 5 ___.   grams   kilograms

3. A watermelon weighs about 8 ___.   grams   kilograms

4. A dog weighs about 25 ___.   grams   kilograms

5. An egg weighs about 50 ___.   grams   kilograms

6. A bowling ball weighs about 6 ___.   grams   kilograms

▷ Complete.

7. 1 kilogram = _____ grams

8. 4,000 grams = _____ kilograms

9. 5 kilograms = _____ grams

10. 9,000 grams = _____ kilograms

11. 12 kilograms = _____ grams

12. 20,000 grams = _____ kilograms

Using Math

▷ Sharon works after school at the grocery store. When she packs groceries in bags, she needs to think about the weight of each item. The bags the store uses can only hold up to 5 kilograms in weight. Look at the list of items and their weights. Can Sharon put all the items in one bag?

Work here.

Circle **yes** or **no**.   **Yes**   **No**

Item	Weight
1 loaf of bread	400 grams
1 jar of peanut butter	500 grams
5 apples	1 kilogram
A large bunch of bananas	2 kilograms
1 box of cereal	250 grams

Problem Solving

Choose an Operation

The longest word in the English language has 34 letters. The longest Swedish word has 130 letters. How many more letters are in the Swedish word than in the English word?

$$\begin{array}{r} 130 \\ + 34 \\ \hline 164 \end{array} \text{ letters}$$

$$\begin{array}{r} 130 \\ - 34 \\ \hline 96 \end{array} \text{ letters}$$

$$\begin{array}{r} 130 \\ \times\ 34 \\ \hline 4{,}420 \end{array} \text{ letters}$$

$$34 \overline{)130} \quad 3 \text{ R } 28 \text{ letters}$$

> Add to put things together.
> Subtract to take things away.
> Multiply to combine groups.
> Divide to separate groups.

Guided Practice

▶ Ring the correct problem.

1. The first Ferris wheel had 36 cars. Each car could hold 60 people. How many people could ride on the Ferris wheel at one time?

$$\begin{array}{r} 36 \\ + 60 \\ \hline 96 \end{array} \text{ people}$$

$$\begin{array}{r} 60 \\ - 36 \\ \hline 24 \end{array} \text{ people}$$

$$\begin{array}{r} 36 \\ \times\ 60 \\ \hline 2{,}160 \end{array} \text{ people}$$

$$36 \overline{)60} \quad 1 \text{ R } 24 \text{ people}$$

2. Mr. Green placed 2 lamps in his living room. A 100-watt bulb is in one lamp and a 50-watt bulb is in the other. What is the total number of watts in these bulbs?

$$\begin{array}{r} 100 \\ + 50 \\ \hline 150 \end{array} \text{ watts}$$

$$\begin{array}{r} 100 \\ - 50 \\ \hline 50 \end{array} \text{ watts}$$

$$\begin{array}{r} 100 \\ \times\ 50 \\ \hline 5{,}000 \end{array} \text{ watts}$$

$$50 \overline{)100} \quad 2 \text{ watts}$$

Practice

▷ Ring the correct problem.

1. Ms. Martinez bought two space heaters. One of them has a power
   output of 21,000 BTUs, and the other has an output of 36,500 BTUs.
   What is the total output of the two heaters?

21,000	36,500	21,000	1 R 15,500 BTUs
+ 36,500	− 21,000	× 36,500	21,000) 36,500
57,500 BTUs	15,500 BTUs	766,500,000 BTUs	

2. Micki works 25 hours each week. She works 50 weeks
   each year. How many hours each year does Micki work?

25	50	50	2 hours
+ 50	− 25	× 25	25) 50
75 hours	25 hours	1,250 hours	

3. Mr. Hong bought movie tickets for the 28 students in his class.
   He spent $168 on tickets. How much did each ticket cost?

$168	$168	$ 168	$ 6 each
+ 28	− 28	× 28	28) $168
$196 each	$140 each	$4,704 each	

4. There are 1,263 students at West High School.
   There are 804 students at Central High.
   How many more students are there at West than at Central?

1,263	1,263	1,263	1 R 459 more
+ 804	− 804	× 804	804) 1,263
2,067 more	459 more	1,015,452 more	

CHAPTER 7 Review

Write the ratio as a fraction in lowest terms. pages 138–139

1. 1 ruler to 2 students

2. 5 school days to 7 days

3. 9 inches to 12 inches ☐ = ☐

4. 22 pencils to 25 pens

5. 4 hours to 24 hours ☐ = ☐

6. 9 tomatoes to 8 cucumbers

Write each ratio as a percent. pages 140–141

7. $\dfrac{19}{100}$ = _____

8. $\dfrac{55}{100}$ = _____

9. $\dfrac{7}{100}$ = _____

Write each percent as a ratio.

10. 85% = ☐

11. 1% = ☐

12. 60% = ☐

Complete. Then write each ratio as a percent. pages 142–143

13. $\dfrac{1}{50} = \dfrac{1 \times \square}{50 \times \square} = \dfrac{\square}{100}$ = _____

14. $\dfrac{3}{10} = \dfrac{3 \times \square}{10 \times \square} = \dfrac{\square}{100}$ = _____

15. $\dfrac{2}{25} = \dfrac{2 \times \square}{25 \times \square} = \dfrac{\square}{\square}$ = _____

16. $\dfrac{2}{5} = \dfrac{2 \times \square}{5 \times \square} = \dfrac{\square}{\square}$ = _____

154

▷Write each decimal as a percent. pages 144–145

17. 0.49 = _____

18. 0.05 = _____

19. 0.25 = _____

▷Write each percent as a decimal.

20. 64% = _____

21. 12% = _____

22. 1% = _____

▷Complete the chart. Round each decimal to the nearest hundredth. pages 146–147

Fraction	Decimal	Percent
$\frac{1}{5}$	23. _____	24. _____
$\frac{3}{4}$	25. _____	26. _____
$\frac{3}{7}$	27. _____	28. _____

▷Find the percent of each number. pages 148–149

29. 20% of 45 = _____

30. 3% of 60 = _____

31. 33% of 100 = _____

32. 25% of 55 = _____

33. 90% of 18 = _____

34. 9% of 34 = _____

35. 10% of 70 = _____

36. 50% of 90 = _____

37. 75% of 30 = _____

38. 12% of 125 = _____

▷Complete. pages 150–151

39. 6 kilograms = _____ grams

40. 7,000 grams = _____ kilograms

41. 17,000 grams = _____ kilograms

42. 2,000 grams = _____ kilograms

43. 11 kilograms = _____ grams

44. 1 kilogram = _____ grams

155

CHAPTER 7 Review

▷ Ring the correct problem.   pages 152–153

45. A yo-yo factory makes 180 yo-yos every minute.

    There are 60 minutes in an hour.

    How many yo-yos does the factory make in 1 hour?

180	180	180	3 yo-yos
+ 60	− 60	× 60	60) 180
240 yo-yos	120 yo-yos	10,800 yo-yos	

46. Ms. Taylor was born in 1948. Ms. Sun was born in 1953.

    How many years older is Ms. Taylor than Ms. Sun?

1953	1953	1953	1 R 5 years
+ 1948	− 1948	× 1948	1948) 1953
3,901 years	5 years	3,804,444 years	

47. There are 246 calories in 3 ounces of broiled ground beef.

    How many calories are in 1 ounce of ground beef?

246	246	246	82 calories
+ 3	− 3	× 3	3) 246
249 calories	243 calories	738 calories	

48. Jeff spent $27.00 on concert tickets. He spent $19.00 on a radio.

    How much in all did Jeff spend?

$27.00	$27.00	$ 27.00	$ 1.42
+ $19.00	− $19.00	× $ 19.00	$19.00) $27.00
$46.00	$ 8.00	$513.00	

156

▷ Write the ratio as a fraction in lowest terms.

1. 1 cat to 5 dogs ☐

2. 6 months to 12 months ☐ = ☐

▷ Write each ratio as a percent and each percent as a ratio.

3. $\dfrac{35}{100}$ = _____

4. $\dfrac{70}{100}$ = _____

5. 18% = ☐

6. 40% = ☐

▷ Complete. Then write each ratio as a percent.

7.

$$\dfrac{3}{25} = \dfrac{3 \times \boxed{}}{25 \times \boxed{}} = \dfrac{\boxed{}}{100} = \underline{\qquad}$$

8.

$$\dfrac{1}{2} = \dfrac{1 \times \boxed{}}{2 \times \boxed{}} = \boxed{} = \underline{\qquad}$$

▷ Write each decimal as a percent and each percent as a decimal.

9. 0.38 = _____

10. 0.06 = _____

11. 75% = _____

12. 3% = _____

▷ Complete the chart.

Fraction	Decimal	Percent
$\dfrac{1}{4}$	13. _____	14. _____

▷ Find the percent of each number.

15. 10% of 50 = _____

16. 45% of 70 = _____

▷ Complete.

17. 1,000 grams = _____ kilogram

18. 7 kilograms = _____ grams **157**

▶ Ring the correct problem.

19. Mr. Weeks sold parrots for $184 each. He sold 8 parrots.

    How much money in all did Mr. Weeks make from these sales?

$184	$184	$ 184	$ 23 in all
+ 8	− 8	× 8	8) $184
$192 in all	$176 in all	$1,472 in all	

---

20. In one week Gina spent 28 hours at the gym lifting weights.

    She spent the same number of hours each day at the gym.

    She went to the gym 7 days that week. How many hours did

    Gina spend at the gym each day?

28	28	28	4 hours
+ 7	− 7	× 7	7) 28
35 hours	21 hours	196 hours	

---

21. Jerry spent 55 minutes working math problems.

    He spent 39 minutes answering questions on a reading assignment.

    How many minutes did Jerry spend on his homework?

55	55	55	1 R 16 minutes
+ 39	− 39	× 39	39) 55
94 minutes	16 minutes	2,145 minutes	

---

22. Carrie planned to take a trip that was 480 miles. She stopped at a hotel

    after driving 120 miles. How many more miles did Carrie have to drive?

480	480	480	4 miles
+ 120	− 120	× 120	120) 480
600 miles	360 miles	57,600 miles	

▷Multiply. pages 72–77

1. $\begin{array}{r} 0.2\,3 \\ \times\quad 3 \\ \hline \end{array}$	2. $\begin{array}{r} 0.4\,1\,3 \\ \times\quad 6 \\ \hline \end{array}$	3. $\begin{array}{r} 5\,6.2 \\ \times\quad 0.9 \\ \hline \end{array}$	4. $\begin{array}{r} 4.0\,3 \\ \times\quad 0.7 \\ \hline \end{array}$	5. $\begin{array}{r} 6.9\,8 \\ \times\quad 0.4 \\ \hline \end{array}$
6. $\begin{array}{r} 6\,3.2 \\ \times\quad 1.2 \\ \hline \end{array}$	7. $\begin{array}{r} 6.0\,8 \\ \times\quad 5.2 \\ \hline \end{array}$	8. $\begin{array}{r} 2\,7.6 \\ \times\quad 8.6 \\ \hline \end{array}$	9. $\begin{array}{r} 0.0\,4 \\ \times\quad 0.2 \\ \hline \end{array}$	10. $\begin{array}{r} 0.0\,3 \\ \times\quad 0.9 \\ \hline \end{array}$

▷Divide. pages 78–83

11. $8\overline{)1\,2.8}$	12. $4\overline{)2.6}$	13. $1\,8\overline{)7\,6.5}$	14. $0.8\overline{)0.7\,2}$
15. $3.4\overline{)8.8\,4}$	16. $2.3\overline{)3\,2.2}$	17. $0.0\,6\overline{)0.5\,5\,8}$	18. $0.4\,7\overline{)7.5\,2}$

▷Complete. pages 84–85

19. 304 milliliters = _____ liters

20. 1.11 liters = _____ milliliters

▷ Write an equivalent fraction. pages 96–97

1. $\frac{1}{7} = \frac{1 \times 2}{7 \times 2} = $ ☐

2. $\frac{3}{8} = \frac{3 \times 3}{8 \times 3} = $ ☐

3. $\frac{4}{5} = \frac{4 \times 4}{5 \times 4} = $ ☐

▷ Complete to reduce each fraction to lowest terms. pages 98–99

4. $\frac{4}{8} = \frac{4 \div \boxed{}}{8 \div \boxed{}} = $ ☐

5. $\frac{3}{12} = \frac{3 \div \boxed{}}{12 \div \boxed{}} = $ ☐

6. $\frac{10}{15} = \frac{10 \div \boxed{}}{15 \div \boxed{}} = $ ☐

▷ Compare the fractions. Write >, <, or = in the box. pages 100–101

7. $\frac{3}{7}$ ☐ $\frac{6}{7}$

8. $\frac{1}{4}$ ☐ $\frac{5}{6}$

▷ Change each improper fraction to a whole number or mixed number. pages 102–103

9. $\frac{7}{4} = $ _____

10. $\frac{16}{4} = $ _____

11. $\frac{9}{2} = $ _____

▷ Change each fraction or mixed number to a decimal. pages 104–105

12. $\frac{7}{10} = $ _____

13. $\frac{4}{5} = $ _____

14. $3\frac{1}{2} = $ _____

▷ Complete. pages 106–107

15. 4 pints = _____ quarts

16. 2 gallons = _____ quarts

▷ Round to the nearest whole number.

Estimate to solve. pages 86–87

1. Tori has 5 packages to
    mail. Each package costs $12.34
    to mail. About how much will
    it cost Tori to mail the packages?

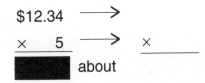

about _____

2. Murry spent $15.87 on cookies. He
    He bought 8 boxes. About how
    much did each box of cookies cost?

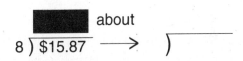

about _____

▷ Cross out the fact you do not need.

Then solve the problem. pages 108–109

3. In Mr. Kite's class, $\frac{4}{8}$ of the students like to play soccer. $\frac{1}{8}$ of the students like to play baseball. $\frac{3}{8}$ of the students like to play football. Do more students like to play soccer or baseball? more like _____.	4. $\frac{1}{4}$ of Ms. Garza's books are mysteries. $\frac{1}{4}$ of her books are old textbooks. $\frac{2}{4}$ of her books are comedies. Does Ms. Garza have more old textbooks or more comedies? more _____
5. Tammy made an apple pie. Her family ate $\frac{6}{12}$ of the pie. She gave a friend $\frac{2}{12}$ of the pie. She saved $\frac{4}{12}$ of the pie. Did Tammy's family or Tammy's friend eat more pie? Tammy's _____ ate more.	6. Max roller skated $\frac{3}{6}$ of the day on Saturday. He also ran $\frac{1}{2}$ mile. He roller skated $\frac{2}{6}$ of the day on Sunday. Did Max roller skate longer on Saturday or on Sunday? more on _____

▷Add or subtract. Reduce your answer to lowest terms.   pages 116–119

1.
$$\frac{1}{4}$$
$$+\ \frac{1}{4}$$

[ ] = [ ]

2.
$$\frac{5}{8}$$
$$+\ \frac{1}{8}$$

[ ] = [ ]

3.
$$\frac{5}{6}$$
$$-\ \frac{1}{6}$$

[ ] = [ ]

4.
$$\frac{7}{9}$$
$$-\ \frac{4}{9}$$

[ ] = [ ]

▷Add or subtract. Reduce the sum or difference to lowest terms.

pages 120–123
5.
$$\frac{1}{2} = [\ ]$$
$$+\ \frac{3}{4} = [\ ]$$

[ ] = [ ]

6.
$$\frac{5}{6} = [\ ]$$
$$+\ \frac{2}{3} = [\ ]$$

[ ] = [ ] = [ ]

7.
$$\frac{3}{4} = [\ ]$$
$$-\ \frac{3}{8} = [\ ]$$

[ ]

pages 124–127
8.
$$3\frac{1}{4}$$
$$+\ 1\frac{1}{4}$$

[ ] = [ ]

9.
$$9\frac{7}{8}$$
$$-\ 6\frac{5}{8}$$

[ ] = [ ]

10.
$$7\frac{1}{4} = [\ ]$$
$$-\ 3\frac{1}{8} = [\ ]$$

[ ]

▷Complete.   pages 128–129

11. **6 tons** = _____ **pounds**

12. **32 ounces** = _____ **pounds**

▷ Write the ratio as a fraction in lowest terms. pages 138–139

1. 1 car to 4 people ☐

2. 2 years to 6 years ☐ = ☐

▷ Write each ratio as a percent and each percent as a ratio. pages 140–141

3. $\frac{62}{100}$ = _____

4. $\frac{8}{100}$ = _____

5. 50% = ☐

6. 9% = ☐

▷ Complete. Then write each ratio as a percent. pages 142–143

7. $\frac{3}{50} = \frac{3 \times \boxed{}}{50 \times \boxed{}} = \frac{\boxed{}}{\boxed{}}$ = _____

8. $\frac{1}{4} = \frac{1 \times \boxed{}}{4 \times \boxed{}} = \frac{\boxed{}}{\boxed{}}$ = _____

▷ Write each decimal as a percent and each percent as a decimal. pages 144–145

9. 0.17 = _____

10. 0.03 = _____

11. 39% = _____

12. 4% = _____

▷ Complete. pages 146–147

Fraction	Decimal	Percent
$\frac{1}{2}$	13. _____	14. _____

▷ Find the percent of each number. pages 148–149

15. 10% of 30 = _____

16. 15% of 80 = _____

▷ Complete. pages 150–151

17. 4,000 grams = _____ kilograms

18. 17 kilograms = _____ grams

163

▶ Cross out the fact you do not need.
Then solve the problem. pages 130–131

<table>
<tr><td>

1. Frank spends $\frac{1}{3}$ of his day in school and $\frac{1}{3}$ of his day at work. He spends $\frac{1}{6}$ of his time at school in band. What part of the day does Frank spend in school and at work?

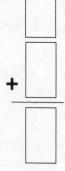

day

</td><td>

2. Rita rode her bike $\frac{4}{8}$ of a mile to the music store. She then rode $\frac{3}{8}$ of a mile to the pool. She was gone for $\frac{5}{8}$ of the day. How much farther did Rita ride to the music store than she rode to the pool?

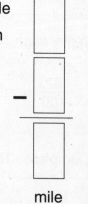

mile

</td></tr>
</table>

▶ Ring the correct problem. pages 152–153

3. The Keep Downtown Beautiful Committee is planting 54 shrubs an equal distance apart. They will plant them along a curb that is 162 yards long. How many yards apart will the committee plant the shrubs?

$$\begin{array}{r} 162 \\ +\ 54 \\ \hline 216 \end{array} \text{ yards} \qquad \begin{array}{r} 162 \\ -\ 54 \\ \hline 108 \end{array} \text{ yards} \qquad \begin{array}{r} 162 \\ \times\ 54 \\ \hline 8{,}748 \end{array} \text{ yards} \qquad 54\overline{)162}^{\,3 \text{ yards}}$$

4. George scored 12 touchdowns for his football team. Each touchdown is worth 6 points. How many points did he score from touchdowns?

$$\begin{array}{r} 12 \\ +\ 6 \\ \hline 18 \end{array} \text{ points} \qquad \begin{array}{r} 12 \\ -\ 6 \\ \hline 6 \end{array} \text{ points} \qquad \begin{array}{r} 12 \\ \times\ 6 \\ \hline 72 \end{array} \text{ points} \qquad 6\overline{)12}^{\,2 \text{ points}}$$

Extra Practice

▷ Write each number. pages 2–3

1. 19 thousand, 362 _____

2. 5 million, 396 thousand, 27 _____

▷ Add. pages 4–7

3.	4.	5.	6.
1 0 7 +6 4 9	2,9 7 6 +4,8 9 3	7 2,6 8 4 +1 1 7,9 0 9	2 8 6,9 7 1 + 9 8,4 8 6

▷ Subtract. pages 8–11

7.	8.	9.	10.
7 2 4 −6 9 1	7,7 9 6 −4,8 9 3	3,0 0 0 −1,2 2 6	4 0,0 0 3 −1 7,6 5 1

▷ Estimate each sum or difference by rounding the numbers to the place shown. pages 12–13

11.	**Nearest Hundred**	12.	**Nearest Thousand**
6,8 3 9 ⟶ +4,7 7 5 ⟶ + _____		5 5,1 2 7 ⟶ −1 4,9 8 2 ⟶ − _____	

▷ Circle the correct temperature. pages 14–15

13. Your body temperature is normal.	14. You go swimming on Saturday.
32°F 200°F 98°F	91°F 15°F 49°F

▶Multiply.

pages 24–27

1. 41 × 2	2. 37 ×40	3. 99 ×12	4. 68 ×32	5. 615 × 23

▶Divide. pages 28–31

6. 2)24	7. 3)56	8. 4)128	9. 9)465
10. 21)89	11. 43)734	12. 33)99	13. 14)729

▶Complete. pages 36–37

14. 108 inches = _____ feet

15. 15 feet = _____ yards

16. 2 miles = _____ feet

17. 12 inches = _____ foot

18. 13 yards = _____ inches

19. 4 feet = _____ inches

166

Use two steps to solve. pages 16–17

	Step 1	Step 2
1. Karen's photo album holds 285 pictures. She has 72 pictures from her trip to Hawaii. She has 24 pictures from the talent show. How many more pictures can Karen put in her album?		**more**
2. Keith polled 537 students to find out how they felt about a plan to limit student parking. 434 students were against the plan. 56 students were undecided. How many students were for the plan?		**students**

Use two steps to solve. pages 38–39

	Step 1	Step 2
3. There were 132 students registered to take an art class. The teacher taught the class at 6 different times. He put the students into equal groups. He taught 4 of the classes on Monday. How many students did he teach on Monday?		**students**
4. It took Rolando 45 minutes to run 5 miles. How many minutes will it take him to run 8 miles if he keeps running the same speed?		**minutes**

Extra Practice

Write each decimal. pages 46–49

1. 13 hundredths = _____

2. 8 and 14 thousandths = _____

Compare. Write >, <, or = . pages 50–51

3. 0.1 _____ 0.2

4. 0.2 _____ 0.20

5. 3.79 _____ 3.68

Add. Write one or more zeros if needed. pages 52–53

6.	7.	8.	9.	10.
0.5 +0.5	7.6 4 + 3.5 2	1.8 +0.7 6	1.5 7 +1.4	3.4 6 3 +3.2

Subtract. Write one or more zeros if needed. pages 54–55

11.	12.	13.	14.	15.
0.9 −0.5	2.3 7 −0.8 9	4.7 2 9 −3.1 8 6	5.9 −0.7 6	9 −4.1 9

Round to the nearest place. pages 56–57

16. **whole number**	17. **tenth**	18. **hundredth**
7.6 _____	0.12 _____	9.035 _____

Complete. pages 58–59

19. 300 centimeters = _____ meters

20. 21 kilometers = _____ meters

21. 5,000 meters = _____ kilometers

22. 10 meters = _____ centimeters

168

▷Multiply. pages 72–77

1. 0.3 4 × 2	2. 0.7 3 1 × 7	3. 6 5.2 × 0.6	4. 7.0 7 × 0.4	5. 3.9 8 × 0.5
6. 1 6.5 × 1.9	7. 4.0 3 × 5.2	8. 1 7.6 × 8.4	9. 0.0 2 × 0.4	10. 0.0 3 × 0.2

▷Divide. pages 78–83

11. 3)5.1	12. 6)1.5	13. 1 8)6 2.1	14. 0.8)0.4 8
15. 1.4)8.6 8	16. 2.3)3 2.2	17. 0.0 3)0.1 4 4	18. 0.3 7)5.5 5

▷Complete. pages 84–85

19. 136 milliliters = _____ liters   20. 7.5 liters = _____ milliliters   **169**

▷Round to the nearest thousand.

Estimate to solve. pages 60–61

1. Liza scored 77,658 points on a video game. Reba scored 45,732 points on the same game. About how many more points did Liza score than Reba?

$$77,658 \longrightarrow$$
$$- 45,732 \longrightarrow -$$

about _____ points

2. There were 4,589 people at the fair on Saturday. There were 3,924 people there on Sunday. About how many people in all went to the fair these days?

$$4,589 \longrightarrow$$
$$+ 3,924 \longrightarrow +$$

about _____ people

▷Round to the nearest dollar.

Estimate to solve. pages 86–87

3. A book cost $4.36. Ms. Newby bought 5 copies of the same book for her classroom. About how much did Ms. Newby spend on books?

$$\$4.36 \longrightarrow$$
$$\times \ 5 \longrightarrow \times$$

about

4. Gail spent $12.18 on 4 pounds of mixed nuts. About how much did each pound of nuts cost?

about

$$4 \overline{)\ \$12.18} \longrightarrow \overline{)}$$

Write an equivalent fraction.   pages 96–97

1. $\dfrac{2}{3} = \dfrac{2 \times 2}{3 \times 2} = \boxed{}$	2. $\dfrac{3}{7} = \dfrac{3 \times 3}{7 \times 3} = \boxed{}$	3. $\dfrac{2}{9} = \dfrac{2 \times 2}{9 \times 2} = \boxed{}$

Complete to reduce each fraction to lowest terms.   pages 98–99

4. $\dfrac{6}{10} = \dfrac{6 \div \boxed{}}{10 \div \boxed{}} = \boxed{}$	5. $\dfrac{4}{12} = \dfrac{4 \div \boxed{}}{12 \div \boxed{}} = \boxed{}$	6. $\dfrac{8}{16} = \dfrac{8 \div \boxed{}}{16 \div \boxed{}} = \boxed{}$

Compare the fractions. Write >, <, or = in the box.   pages 100–101

7. $\dfrac{4}{5} \ \boxed{} \ \dfrac{7}{5}$	8. $\dfrac{3}{6} \ \boxed{} \ \dfrac{1}{2}$

Change each improper fraction to a whole number or mixed number.   pages 102–103

9. $\dfrac{9}{5} = $ _____	10. $\dfrac{12}{3} = $ _____	11. $\dfrac{16}{7} = $ _____

Change each fraction or mixed number to a decimal.   pages 104–105

12. $\dfrac{2}{10} = $ _____	13. $\dfrac{1}{4} = $ _____	14. $3\dfrac{3}{5} = $ _____

Complete.   pages 106–107

15. 4 gallons = _____ quarts

16. 8 pints = _____ gallon

▶ Add or subtract. Reduce your answer to lowest terms.   pages 116–119

1.
$$\frac{1}{2}$$
$$+\ \frac{1}{2}$$
[ ] = [ ]

2.
$$\frac{3}{7}$$
$$+\ \frac{1}{7}$$
[ ]

3.
$$\frac{2}{3}$$
$$-\ \frac{1}{3}$$
[ ]

4.
$$\frac{7}{6}$$
$$-\ \frac{3}{6}$$
[ ] = [ ]

▶ Add or subtract. Reduce the sum or difference to lowest terms.

pages 120–123

5.
$$\frac{3}{8} = [\ ]$$
$$+\ \frac{1}{4} = [\ ]$$
[ ]

6.
$$\frac{4}{6} = [\ ]$$
$$+\ \frac{1}{3} = [\ ]$$
[ ] = [ ]

7.
$$\frac{1}{2} = [\ ]$$
$$-\ \frac{1}{4} = [\ ]$$
[ ]

8.
$$\frac{4}{5} = [\ ]$$
$$-\ \frac{2}{10} = [\ ]$$
[ ] = [ ]

pages 124–127

9.
$$2\frac{1}{2} = [\ ]$$
$$+\ 3\frac{1}{4} = [\ ]$$
[ ]

10.
$$9\frac{5}{9}$$
$$-\ 6\frac{2}{9}$$
[ ] = [ ]

11.
$$7\frac{5}{6} = [\ ]$$
$$-\ 1\frac{1}{3} = [\ ]$$
[ ] = [ ]

▶ Complete.   pages 128–129

12. 2 tons = _____ pounds

13. 208 ounces = _____ pounds

14. 8 pounds = _____ ounces

15. 9 tons = _____ pounds

172

▷ Write the ratio as a fraction in lowest terms. pages 138-139

1. 1 hat to 5 coats ☐

2. 1 gallon to 20 miles ☐

▷ Write each ratio as a percent and each percent as a ratio. pages 140-141

3. $\dfrac{20}{100}$ = _____

4. $\dfrac{9}{100}$ = _____

5. 3% = ☐

6. 76% = ☐

▷ Complete. Then write each ratio as a percent. pages 142-143

7.	8.
$\dfrac{4}{10} = \dfrac{4 \times \boxed{}}{10 \times \boxed{}} = \boxed{\dfrac{}{}}$ = _____	$\dfrac{1}{4} = \dfrac{1 \times \boxed{}}{4 \times \boxed{}} = \boxed{\dfrac{}{}}$ = _____

▷ Write each decimal as a percent and each percent as a decimal. pages 144-145

9. 0.42 = _____

10. 0.08 = _____

11. 53% = _____

12. 1% = _____

▷ Complete. pages 146-147

Fraction	Decimal	Percent
$\dfrac{1}{5}$	13. _____	14. _____

▷ Find the percent of each number. pages 148-149

15. 50% of 200 = _____

16. 65% of 90 = _____

▷ Complete. pages 150-151

17. 13,000 grams = _____ kilograms

18. 18 kilograms = _____ grams

▷Cross out the fact you do not need.

Then solve the problem. pages 108–109

1. Jason spent $\frac{5}{8}$ of an hour grocery shopping. He spent $\frac{3}{8}$ of an hour at the mall. It took him $\frac{4}{5}$ of an hour to drive home. Did Jason spend more time grocery shopping or at the mall?

more time _____

2. Winona sang $\frac{2}{4}$ hour. Then she played her guitar $\frac{1}{2}$ hour. She played the piano $\frac{1}{4}$ hour. Did Winona spend more time singing or playing the piano?

more time _____

pages 130–131

3. Mr. Jackson drives a truck that will hold $\frac{4}{4}$ tons of freight. Mr. Ritchey's truck will hold $\frac{3}{4}$ tons of freight. Ms. Aguilar's truck will hold $\frac{3}{4}$ tons also. How much more will Mr. Jackson's truck hold than Ms. Aguilar's truck?

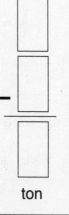

ton

4. Belva's apartment building was painted 3 colors. $\frac{4}{9}$ of the building is blue. $\frac{1}{9}$ of the building is white. $\frac{4}{9}$ of the building is gray. What fraction of the building is blue or gray?

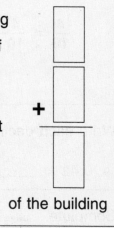

of the building

▷Ring the correct problem. pages 152–153

5. Alvin spent 36 hours working on a science project. He worked 9 hours each week on it. How many weeks in all did it take Alvin to finish his project?

$$\begin{array}{r} 36 \\ + 9 \\ \hline 45 \end{array} \text{ weeks}$$

$$\begin{array}{r} 36 \\ - 9 \\ \hline 27 \end{array} \text{ weeks}$$

$$\begin{array}{r} 36 \\ \times 9 \\ \hline 324 \end{array} \text{ weeks}$$

$$9\overline{)36}\quad\text{4 weeks}$$